MCQ in IoT

For Beginners Volume:- 1 of 3

Prepare for success with IoT multiple choice questions

Dr. Dheeraj Mehrotra
Dr. Brijesh Bakariya

www.bpbonline.com

First Edition 2026

Copyright © BPB Publications, India

ISBN: 978-93-65892-970

To View Complete
BPB Publications Catalogue
Scan the QR Code:

Dedicated to

Our family members who have supported us in all aspects of life and career. Our journey proved to be a boon by following their words and experiences.

About the Authors

- **Dr. Dheeraj Mehrotra**, with an MS, MPhil, and Ph.D. (education management), is also an H.C., a white and yellow belt in Six Sigma, and a certified NLP business diploma holder. He is an educational innovator and author with expertise in Six Sigma in education, academic audits, **neuro-linguistic programming** (**NLP**), and total quality management.

Dr. Mehrotra is also an experiential educator and a CBSE resource for school assessment (SQAA), CCE, JIT, Five S, and Kaizen. He has authored over 100 books on topics including computer science, AI, digital body language, NLP, quality circles, school management, classroom effectiveness, and safety and security in schools.

He is a former principal at De Indian Public School, New Delhi (India), NPS International School, Guwahati, and education officer at GEMS, Gurgaon, with over two decades of teaching experience. He is a certified trainer for quality circles/TQM in education and QCI standards for school accreditation/school audits and management.

He was honored with the president of India's National Teacher Award in 2006, the Best Science Teacher State Award from the Ministry of Science and Technology, Uttar Pradesh, and the Innovation in Education Award for his inception of Six Sigma in Education by Education Watch, New Delhi. He also received the Education World-Best Teacher Award, the BOLT Learner Teacher Award by Air India, and the Innovation in Education Award 2016 by Higher Education Forum (HEF), Gujarat Chapter, among others. He developed over 150 free educational mobile apps for the Google Play Store exclusively for teachers, students, and parents. This work has been recognized by the Limca Book of Records and India Book of Records as the only Indian to achieve that feat. Dr. Mehrotra currently serves as the principal at Kunwars Global School, Lucknow, in India. He has conducted over 1000 workshops globally on excellence in education, integrating total quality management and six sigma, **technology integration in education** (**TIE**), and developing Rockstar Teachers. His workshops cover topics such as cyberspace, cyber security, classroom management, school leadership and management, and innovative teaching within classrooms via Mind Maps, NLP, and experiential learning in academics. He is also an active TEDx speaker, with talks available on the YouTube TEDx channel.

As a premium Udemy instructor, he has developed over 450 courses, serving over 8 Lakh students from 180 countries.

- **Dr. Brijesh Bakariya**, MCA, Ph.D. (computer applications), is an academician, researcher, and author with extensive expertise in data science, artificial intelligence, machine learning, IoT, and programming languages. He is currently serving as an assistant professor in the department of computer science and engineering at I.K. Gujral Punjab Technical University, Hoshiarpur Campus (Punjab, India). With over 15 years of teaching experience, he has contributed significantly to higher education, research supervision, and academic leadership.

He earned his Ph.D. in computer applications from Maulana Azad **National Institute of Technology (NIT)**, Bhopal, 2016, and completed his MCA from DAVV University, Indore, 2009. Over the years, he has supervised and awarded three Ph.D. scholars and is currently guiding several more in cutting-edge areas such as machine learning for healthcare, deep learning-based human activity recognition, and predictive modeling.

His research contributions are remarkable, with more than 40 publications in SCI and Scopus-indexed journals, etc (including Springer, Elsevier, CRC Press, and Bentham Science). His work spans across AI-driven medical diagnosis, sentiment analysis, human activity recognition, weblog analysis, and IoT-based intelligent systems. He has also presented papers at prestigious international and national conferences. He is the author and co-author of multiple books with reputed publishers such as BPB Publications and Springer. He has also contributed book chapters in advanced domains like smart schools, lung cancer detection, and sentiment analysis techniques. A prolific innovator, He has filed and published multiple patents in the domains of data science, clustering, COVID-19 detection via mobile applications, and big data efficiency.

He is an active member of professional bodies such as IRED, IAENG, and SDIWC. Dedicated to continuous learning, He has attended numerous **faculty development programs (FDPs)**, **short-term training programs (STTPs)**, and workshops conducted by IITs, NITs, NITTTR, and AICTE across domains like Python, machine learning, deep learning, data science, cloud computing, and cryptography. His professional journey reflects his passion for quality education, research excellence, and innovation in technology integration. His commitment to advancing computer science education and guiding the next generation of researchers continues to inspire students, peers, and the academic community at large.

About the Reviewers

❖ **Rakesh Kumar Pal** is a highly experienced technology leader with over two decades of progressive experience in pre-sales, customer success, project management, AI/ML, cloud computing design/architecture, implementation, and cloud and DevSecOps solutions. Rakesh brings a high-energy, people-centric approach, combining creative thinking with a collaborative management style. He is renowned for delivering error-free, efficient services and applications that consistently pass rigorous testing, on-time, and within budget, offering a unique blend of technical skills and diverse industry experience.

He is currently working in Amazon and part of the cloud solution team.

❖ **Banani Mohapatra** is an AI/ML data science leader at Walmart, operating at the intersection of product development and applied AI. She shapes strategy from inception to launch through machine learning, causal inference, and experimental design. With over 13 years of experience spanning e-commerce (Walmart), payments (Visa), and real estate (Realtor. com), she currently leads a global team of more than 25 data scientists and data engineers at Walmart. She has led cutting-edge research to accelerate the adoption of Walmart Labs' subscription products by applying AI across the customer journey - including advanced item recommendation systems, IoT-powered personalized content generation for user engagement, and creative optimization for marketing campaigns. These initiatives have resulted in more relevant experiences for millions of customers and contributed directly to subscription growth and operational efficiency.

❖ **Abhishek Arya** is a seasoned solutions architect and technology leader with over two decades of experience delivering innovative IoT, cloud, data, and AI solutions across industries including retail, finance, telecom, and supply chain. He specializes in designing scalable, secure, and high-performance IoT architectures using leading cloud platforms such as AWS, Azure, Google Cloud Platform, and Microsoft Fabric. His expertise spans the complete IoT ecosystem, from edge device integration and data ingestion to real-time analytics and cloud-based insights, empowering organizations to accelerate digital transformation through connected technologies. A notable achievement includes developing an NHVR (Australia)-compliant driver fatigue management algorithm, leveraging advanced sensor data, AI models, and regulatory logic to enhance transport safety and compliance.

Abhishek is proficient in modern architecture paradigms, including microservices, serverless computing, containerization, DevSecOps, CI/CD automation, and infrastructure as code. With deep expertise in data lake architecture, streaming pipelines, and AI/ML frameworks like GPT-4, Hugging Face, and LangChain, he consistently delivers intelligent, data-driven insights from complex IoT ecosystems while optimizing cloud spend and leading global teams. He is a member of a non-profit organisation contributing to the innovation and growth of AI and IoT solutions in India and has published various articles on IoT, blockchain, and AI across both digital and print media, establishing himself as a thought leader who aligns technology strategies with business objectives for measurable impact.

❖ **Shreya Solanke** is a passionate IoT engineer and leader with extensive professional experience in the domain of IoT, IoT devices, IoT communication stacks, wireless short range radio protocols, IIoT, building controller and EMS ecosystems. Shreya specializes in IoT devices integration to the cloud through multiple patterns and multiple diverse range of devices. She has an extensive with IoT platforms like Microsoft Azure, ThingWorx, AWS, Thingsboard etc. She is an active contributor in two of the IEEE standards P2994 and P1931.1

Acknowledgements

This book culminates a few years of intense learning and research experience. We have been fortunate to interact with many people who have influenced us greatly. One of the pleasures of finally finishing the book is this opportunity to thank them. We would like to place on record and acknowledge the works of all those great authors whose work we have referred to in preparing this book.

We want to thank a few people for the continued and ongoing support they have given us while writing this book. First and foremost, we would like to thank our family members for continuously encouraging us to write the book; we could never have completed this book without their support.

We are also grateful to BPB Publications for their guidance and expertise in bringing this book to fruition. Revising this book was a long journey, with the valuable participation and collaboration of reviewers, technical experts, and editors.

We would also like to acknowledge the valuable contributions of our colleagues and co-workers during many years working in academia, who have taught us so much and provided valuable feedback on this work.

Finally, we would like to thank all the readers who have taken an interest in our book and for their support in making it a reality. Your encouragement has been invaluable.

Preface

This book emphasizes mastering the key concepts, technologies, and applications in the **Internet of Things (IoT)** through targeted multiple-choice questions.

This volume examines the introduction and foundational elements in IoT, domain-specific IoT, sensors and actuators, and IoT applications, while refining your skills for success in the rapidly evolving IoT domain. This book contains more than 1200 MCQ questions and answer keys. These questions and answers serve as an effective means to assess your proficiency in IoT. If you possess prior knowledge of IoT concepts, you can utilize this book to determine how many questions you can attempt independently without external assistance. Before facing academic examinations, competitive tests, or job interviews, it would be highly advisable to review these MCQs. For teachers or trainers instructing IoT, these multiple-choice questions serve as a valuable assessment tool to evaluate the extent to which learners have grasped the material taught. The intended difficulty level of the questions is primarily aimed at beginners in IoT, those who are just starting their journey into IoT systems, applications, and integration, or those who have recently acquired foundational knowledge of IoT. Each question is accompanied by an answer key for self-assessment.

The book is divided into six chapters, covering MCQs from all aspects of IoT problem-solving, with special emphasis on the introduction, building blocks, domain-specific, sensor, and actuator, and applications to IoT.

Chapter 1: Introduction to IoT- This chapter presents MCQs related to the basic concepts and foundations of the IoT. It covers definitions, evolution, architecture, characteristics, and the overall ecosystem of IoT. Learners will gain clarity on how IoT connects physical devices to the digital world, enabling smart environments and real-time decision-making.

Chapter 2: Building Blocks of IoT- This chapter contains MCQs focused on the essential building blocks of IoT, including hardware (sensors, actuators, microcontrollers), software (middleware, IoT platforms), communication protocols, and cloud integration. These questions highlight how each component plays a role in creating end-to-end IoT systems.

Chapter 3: Domain Specific IoT- This chapter presents MCQs related to various domain-specific applications of IoT, such as healthcare, agriculture, transportation, industrial automation, smart cities, and home automation. It emphasizes the unique requirements, benefits, and challenges of IoT implementation in different sectors.

Chapter 4: Sensor and Actuator- This chapter covers MCQs on sensors and actuators, which serve as the backbone of IoT systems. It explores types of sensors, their working principles, data acquisition methods, and how actuators respond to control signals. These questions strengthen the understanding of how IoT devices sense, interact, and control their environment.

Chapter 5: IoT Applications- This chapter includes MCQs on real-world IoT applications and use cases. It examines how IoT enables smart solutions in everyday life, such as smart homes, wearable devices, intelligent transportation systems, energy management, and industrial IoT. These questions bridge theoretical concepts with practical implementations.

Chapter 6: Interview Questions- This chapter provides beginner-level interview-based MCQs that test fundamental knowledge of IoT. It includes conceptual, technical, and practical questions typically asked during interviews to assess a candidate's basic understanding of IoT, making it a useful resource for students, job seekers, and entry-level professionals.

Errata

We take immense pride in our work at BPB Publications and follow best practices to ensure the accuracy of our content to provide with an indulging reading experience to our subscribers. Our readers are our mirrors, and we use their inputs to reflect and improve upon human errors, if any, that may have occurred during the publishing processes involved. To let us maintain the quality and help us reach out to any readers who might be having difficulties due to any unforeseen errors, please write to us at :

errata@bpbonline.com

Your support, suggestions and feedbacks are highly appreciated by the BPB Publications' Family.

At www.bpbonline.com, you can also read a collection of free technical articles, sign up for a range of free newsletters, and receive exclusive discounts and offers on BPB books and eBooks. You can check our social media handles below:

Instagram

Facebook

Linkedin

YouTube

Get in touch with us at: business@bpbonline.com for more details.

Piracy

If you come across any illegal copies of our works in any form on the internet, we would be grateful if you would provide us with the location address or website name. Please contact us at business@bpbonline.com with a link to the material.

If you are interested in becoming an author

If there is a topic that you have expertise in, and you are interested in either writing or contributing to a book, please visit www.bpbonline.com. We have worked with thousands of developers and tech professionals, just like you, to help them share their insights with the global tech community. You can make a general application, apply for a specific hot topic that we are recruiting an author for, or submit your own idea.

Reviews

Please leave a review. Once you have read and used this book, why not leave a review on the site that you purchased it from? Potential readers can then see and use your unbiased opinion to make purchase decisions. We at BPB can understand what you think about our products, and our authors can see your feedback on their book. Thank you!

For more information about BPB, please visit www.bpbonline.com.

Join our Discord space

Join our Discord workspace for latest updates, offers, tech happenings around the world, new releases, and sessions with the authors:

https://discord.bpbonline.com

Table of Contents

CHAPTER 1
Introduction to IoT

Introduction

Almost every facet of contemporary existence is touched by technology. When talking about this technological revolution, the **Internet of Things (IoT)** is often cited as a key frontier. What exactly is IoT, and why has it become such a popular term in the world of technology? IoT is an interconnected device system that collects and shares data and operates in real time using internet protocols. These things might range from common household appliances like refrigerators and thermostats to sophisticated factory equipment.

IoT is a rapidly evolving technology that enables the interconnection of everyday objects, devices, and systems through the internet, allowing them to collect, exchange, and act on data autonomously. This network of connected devices spans various industries, from smart homes and healthcare to industrial automation and agriculture, driving efficiency, innovation, and new business models. IoT's transformative potential lies in its ability to create intelligent environments where devices communicate seamlessly, providing real-time insights, improving decision-making, and enhancing the overall quality of life.

Past and present

The concept of IoT may seem novel, yet it has really been developing for decades. Despite the idea's antiquity, British businessman *Kevin Ashton* is often credited with coining the term in 1999. IoT first appeared in the early 1990s, when digital sensors were being employed in machines. Nonetheless, technological developments, especially in communication and networking, have opened many opportunities for IoT.

Internet of Things use cases

The breadth of use cases demonstrates the magnitude of IoT:

- Amazon's Alexa and Google's Home have made homes smarter by allowing smart devices to communicate with one another to make daily tasks easier.
- In the medical field, wearable devices may immediately notify physicians of any abnormalities in a patient's vital signs.
- Sensors in the agricultural sector measure soil moisture levels to provide adequate watering of plants.
- IoT is shifting the focus of retail from stock control to customer preference.

Advantages of Internet of Things

These are a few ways that can help us understand the importance of IoT. They are:

- Through the use of interconnected devices, tedious tasks may be automated, such as setting the temperature in the house automatically based on the preferences we teach our smart thermostats.
- Massive amounts of data can be collected and analyzed via the IoT's sensors. Decisions might be enhanced by analyzing this data. By monitoring vital signs, wearable fitness devices empower consumers to make informed decisions about their health.
- IoT has strengthened the economy by optimizing resource utilization, reducing waste, and lowering costs. Not surprisingly, industries, including agriculture, healthcare, and logistics, are eager to adopt IoT technologies.
- The interoperability of IoT devices has significantly improved, enabling seamless data sharing and coordinated outputs.

Disadvantages of Internet of Things

There are some disadvantages to IoT despite its numerous benefits. Let us take a look at them:

- The security risk is higher with more interconnected devices. It is vital that these gadgets and their data be safeguarded.
- Lower to no security controls to safeguard data collected by IoT devices.
- Interoperability among IoT devices manufactured by device manufacturers is a challenge.

Multiple choice questions

1. **What does IoT stand for?**
   a. Internet of Technology
   b. Internet of Things
   c. Internet of Telecommunications
   d. Internet of Techniques

2. **Which of the following is not an example of an IoT device?**
   a. Smartwatch
   b. Refrigerator with Wi-Fi connectivity
   c. Desktop computer
   d. Connected thermostat

3. **What is the fundamental concept behind IoT?**
   a. Connecting people through the internet
   b. Connecting devices to the internet and each other
   c. Connecting only computers to the internet
   d. Connecting devices to a local network

4. **What is the primary goal of IoT devices?**
   a. To perform complex computations
   b. To communicate with each other and with users
   c. To generate electricity
   d. To mimic human behavior

5. **Which statement best describes the smart aspect of IoT devices?**
   a. They can replace humans in decision-making
   b. They can predict future events with high accuracy
   c. They can process and analyze data to make intelligent decisions
   d. They can access the internet without any limitations

6. **What is a sensor in the context of IoT?**
   a. A device that controls other devices remotely
   b. A device that provides connectivity to the internet
   c. A device that measures physical quantities and converts them into digital data
   d. A device that is exclusively used in industrial settings

7. **What is a key challenge associated with IoT security?**
   a. IoT devices are not connected to the internet
   b. IoT devices do not require authentication
   c. IoT devices may lack proper security measures, making them vulnerable
   d. IoT devices can only be accessed by their manufacturers

8. **Which statement best describes the role of data analytics in IoT?**
   a. Data analytics is not relevant in IoT applications
   b. Data analytics is used only for entertainment purposes
   c. Data analytics helps make sense of the massive amounts of data IoT devices generate
   d. Data analytics is limited to financial calculations

9. **Which of the following is an example of an IoT application?**
   a. Cooking a meal
   b. Driving a car
   c. Monitoring room temperature using a smartphone
   d. Watching a movie

10. **What is the potential benefit of IoT in healthcare?**
    a. Making computers faster
    b. Tracking patients' vital signs remotely
    c. Enabling virtual reality gaming
    d. Controlling home appliances using voice commands

11. **Which term refers to devices connected to the internet that can communicate with each other?**
    a. Isolated devices
    b. Offline devices
    c. Smart devices
    d. Disconnected devices

12. **What is one of the goals of IoT implementation?**
    a. Reducing global warming
    b. Increasing air pollution
    c. Enhancing connectivity and convenience
    d. Eliminating the need for human interaction

13. **What role does data play in IoT?**
    a. Data is not relevant in IoT
    b. Data is collected and used for analysis and decision-making
    c. Data is only used for entertainment
    d. Data is not stored in IoT devices

14. **Which of the following is not a characteristic of IoT devices?**
    a. Interconnectivity
    b. Intelligence
    c. Independence
    d. Instrumentation

15. **What is the main purpose of IoT devices?**
    a. Playing video games
    b. Monitoring and controlling physical objects remotely
    c. Sending emails
    d. Creating art

16. **Which technology forms the backbone of IoT communication?**
    a. Satellite communication
    b. Radio waves
    c. Fiber optics
    d. Internet

17. **What does the term smart home refer to in the context of IoT?**
    a. An energy-independent home
    b. A home with advanced security features only
    c. A home where appliances and devices can be controlled remotely
    d. A home built with sustainable materials

18. **Which layer of the IoT architecture deals with aggregating and processing data from various devices?**
    a. Application layer
    b. Network layer
    c. Perception layer
    d. Data layer

19. **Which wireless communication protocol is commonly used for short-range communication between IoT devices?**

    a. Zigbee

    b. 4G LTE

    c. WiMAX

    d. GSM

20. **What does M2M stand for in IoT?**

    a. Made to measure

    b. Machine-to-machine

    c. More to manage

    d. Mind to matter

21. **Which of the following is not a component of the IoT ecosystem?**

    a. Sensors/Devices

    b. Cloud infrastructure

    c. Human brain interface

    d. Data processing and analytics

22. **Which of the following cannot be considered an IoT device?**

    a. Smart watch

    b. Tubelight

    c. Android phone

    d. Laptop

23. **Which of the following is a benefit of IoT implementation?**

    a. Increased complexity of systems

    b. Reduced data collection and analysis

    c. Improved decision-making through data insights

    d. Limited connectivity options

24. **Which security concerns are associated with IoT devices?**

    a. Devices being too expensive

    b. Lack of user interfaces

    c. Data privacy and unauthorized access

    d. Devices being too energy-efficient

25. **What does edge computing refer to in IoT?**
    a. Computing tasks performed by devices at the center of the network
    b. Processing data on the cloud servers
    c. Computing tasks performed by devices at the outer edge of the network
    d. Remote monitoring of devices

26. **Which of the following best describes IoT?**
    a. A network of interconnected laptops and desktops
    b. A network of interconnected humans
    c. A network of interconnected physical devices that communicate and exchange data
    d. A network of interconnected satellites

27. **Which technology is primarily responsible for enabling communication between IoT devices?**
    a. Bluetooth
    b. Wi-Fi
    c. Near Field Communication
    d. All of the above

28. **What is a thing in IoT?**
    a. An intangible concept
    b. Any physical object that can be connected to the internet
    c. A type of software application
    d. A virtual reality simulation

29. **Which of the following is a benefit of using IoT in agriculture?**
    a. Increased manual labor requirements
    b. Reduced water usage through smart irrigation
    c. Decreased use of data analytics for decision-making
    d. Slower response to changing weather conditions

30. **What is the purpose of a sensor in an IoT device?**
    a. To process data
    b. To connect to the internet
    c. To store data
    d. To gather data from the environment

31. What is a smart device in the context of IoT?

    a. A device that can only perform one specific task

    b. A device that can connect to the internet and gather or share data

    c. A device that operates without any form of technology

    d. A device that is only used by tech-savvy individuals

32. What is the role of actuators in IoT systems?

    a. Actuators provide power to IoT devices

    b. Actuators process data collected by sensors

    c. Actuators send and receive data from the cloud

    d. Actuators perform actions based on commands from the cloud or other sources

33. Which of the following is a potential benefit of implementing IoT in industries?

    a. Increased isolation between systems

    b. Reduced need for data analysis

    c. Improved operational efficiency and predictive maintenance

    d. Lower reliance on cloud computing

34. What is the standard form of RFID?

    a. Radio Waves Frequency Identification

    b. Radio Frequency Identification

    c. Radio Frequency Interdependent

    d. Radio Wave Frequency Independent

35. What is considered the standard length for a MAC address?

    a. 8 bits

    b. 32 bits

    c. 48 bits

    d. None of these

36. Which is not a challenge in IoT implementation?

    a. Data security

    b. Interoperability

    c. Lack of IoT platforms

    d. Scalability

37. **Which of these smart homes is an example of in the context of IoT?**

    a. A home with advanced security systems only

    b. A home with connected devices that can be controlled remotely

    c. A home with no technology or devices

    d. A home with manual controls for all appliances

38. **Which of the following is considered one of the first IoT devices?**

    a. Smart watch

    b. Smart refrigerator

    c. Coca-Cola vending machine

    d. Google Home

39. **Which technology is most closely associated with the foundation of IoT?**

    a. Bluetooth

    b. RFID

    c. GPS

    d. Wi-Fi

40. **Which company developed the first IoT platform?**

    a. IBM

    b. Cisco

    c. Microsoft

    d. Google

41. **Which year is considered the birth of the IoT?**

    a. 1989

    b. 1995

    c. 2000

    d. 2008

42. **What was the purpose of the first IoT device created by Carnegie Mellon University?**

    a. To monitor room temperature

    b. To track the stock of Coca-Cola

    c. To control home lighting

    d. To monitor water usage

43. **Which major industry was one of the first to adopt IoT technology?**

    a. Automotive

    b. Agriculture

    c. Healthcare

    d. Manufacturing

44. **Which standard protocol is commonly used in IoT for communication?**

    a. HTTP

    b. MQTT

    c. FTP

    d. SMTP

45. **What is the name of the first consumer IoT product allowing users to remotely monitor and control home appliances?**

    a. Nest Thermostat

    b. Amazon Echo

    c. Philips Hue

    d. SmartThings Hub

46. **Which of the following is a major challenge in IoT?**

    a. High internet speeds

    b. Device interoperability

    c. Abundance of standards

    d. Large storage capacity

47. **What is a common issue with the power consumption of IoT devices?**

    a. Too much energy generation

    b. Too low energy consumption

    c. Battery life limitations

    d. Excessive power supply

48. **Which aspect of IoT is considered a challenge due to the massive data generated?**

    a. Data processing

    b. Data redundancy

    c. Data encryption

    d. Data transmission

49. **Scalability is a challenge in IoT. What does scalability refer to?**
    a. Ability to manage large networks
    b. Ability to maintain device connectivity
    c. Ability to enhance device features
    d. Ability to reduce device costs

50. **Which of the following is a connectivity challenge in IoT?**
    a. Low bandwidth requirements
    b. High latency
    c. Excessive coverage
    d. Minimal network interference

51. **Why is standardization a challenge in IoT?**
    a. Too few IoT devices
    b. Lack of security protocols
    c. Diverse communication protocols
    d. Universal device compatibility

52. **What challenge is associated with the diverse range of IoT devices and manufacturers?**
    a. Homogeneity
    b. Fragmentation
    c. Integration
    d. Uniformity

53. **Which challenge in IoT is associated with ensuring that devices function seamlessly together?**
    a. Data encryption
    b. Device interoperability
    c. Data mining
    d. Device calibration

54. **Which of the following is a challenge concerning the deployment of IoT in rural areas?**
    a. Overcrowded networks
    b. High-speed internet availability
    c. Limited connectivity infrastructure
    d. Abundant technical support

55. What is one of the primary security concerns in IoT?

    a. Excessive data compression

    b. Device misconfiguration

    c. Unauthorized data access

    d. Lack of user interface

56. Which of the following is a common IoT security risk?

    a. Data overloading

    b. Firmware updates

    c. Botnet attacks

    d. User authentication

57. Which type of attack involves taking control of numerous IoT devices to launch a larger attack?

    a. Phishing

    b. Man-in-the-middle

    c. Denial-of-service

    d. Distributed denial-of-service (DDoS)

58. Why are IoT devices particularly vulnerable to cyberattacks?

    a. High processing power

    b. Strong security measures

    c. Limited computing resources

    d. Frequent updates

59. Which IoT security measure involves verifying the identity of devices before they can access the network?

    a. Data encryption

    b. Device authentication

    c. Network segmentation

    d. Anomaly detection

60. Which protocol is commonly used to secure data transmission in IoT?

    a. HTTP

    b. FTP

    c. SSL/TLS

    d. IMAP

61. Which security challenge involves ensuring that data is not altered during transmission?

    a. Data availability

    b. Data integrity

    c. Data redundancy

    d. Data minimization

62. What type of security measure involves regularly updating device firmware to protect against vulnerabilities?

    a. Device calibration

    b. Patch management

    c. Data encryption

    d. Network segmentation

63. Which type of attack involves intercepting and altering communication between IoT devices?

    a. Spoofing

    b. Eavesdropping

    c. Phishing

    d. Man-in-the-middle

64. What is the practice of isolating different parts of a network to enhance security called?

    a. Device authentication

    b. Data encryption

    c. Network segmentation

    d. Patch management

65. Which standard is commonly used for securing IoT devices?

    a. IEEE 802.11

    b. ISO/IEC 27001

    c. Zigbee

    d. Bluetooth

66. **Which of the following best describes a Zero Trust security model?**
    a. Trust but verify
    b. Trust everyone
    c. Never trust, always verify
    d. Verify occasionally

67. **Which IoT security practice involves using cryptographic keys to secure communications?**
    a. Data encryption
    b. Device authentication
    c. Network segmentation
    d. Firmware updates

68. **Why is it important to secure the physical access to IoT devices?**
    a. To prevent software updates
    b. To ensure device connectivity
    c. To prevent tampering or theft
    d. To enhance user experience

69. **Which security measure helps in identifying unauthorized access attempts?**
    a. Patch management
    b. Intrusion detection systems
    c. Data encryption
    d. Device calibration

70. **What is the primary purpose of an IoT security gateway?**
    a. To provide network connectivity
    b. To secure communications between devices
    c. To increase data transmission speed
    d. To monitor device performance

71. **Which of the following is a common security vulnerability in IoT devices?**
    a. Excessive power consumption
    b. Weak default passwords
    c. Limited data storage
    d. High processing power

72. **Why is encryption critical for IoT security?**

    a. To reduce data redundancy

    b. To ensure data confidentiality

    c. To enhance device compatibility

    d. To increase network speed

73. **Which security challenge involves ensuring the availability of IoT services at all times?**

    a. Data integrity

    b. Data encryption

    c. Service availability

    d. Network segmentation

74. **What is the primary role of an IoT device management platform in security?**

    a. To monitor network traffic

    b. To update device firmware

    c. To control device access and permissions

    d. To analyze data patterns

75. **Which of the following helps in protecting IoT devices from malware?**

    a. Device authentication

    b. Antivirus software

    c. Data encryption

    d. Firmware updates

76. **What is the impact of a DoS attack on IoT devices?**

    a. Data corruption

    b. Device malfunction

    c. Service disruption

    d. Unauthorized access

77. **Which security measure involves creating isolated environments for running IoT applications?**

    a. Network segmentation

    b. Sandboxing

    c. Data encryption

    d. Patch management

78. **Why is it important to regularly update the firmware of IoT devices?**

    a. To enhance device features

    b. To fix security vulnerabilities

    c. To increase data storage

    d. To reduce power consumption

79. **Which of the following is a method to ensure the authenticity of IoT devices?**

    a. Data encryption

    b. Device calibration

    c. Digital certificates

    d. Patch management

80. **Which security principle involves limiting access to only those resources needed for a specific function?**

    a. Least privilege

    b. Data encryption

    c. Network segmentation

    d. Device authentication

81. **What is the role of a firewall in IoT security?**

    a. To encrypt data

    b. To control incoming and outgoing network traffic

    c. To authenticate devices

    d. To update firmware

82. **Which type of security attack aims to overload IoT devices with excessive requests?**

    a. Phishing

    b. Man-in-the-middle

    c. DoS/DDoS attacks

    d. Spoofing

83. **What is the significance of using strong, unique passwords for IoT devices?**

    a. To reduce power consumption

    b. To prevent unauthorized access

    c. To enhance data transmission speed

    d. To increase device compatibility

84. **Which security practice involves regular monitoring and analysis of IoT network traffic?**

    a. Patch management

    b. Intrusion detection and prevention

    c. Data encryption

    d. Device calibration

85. **Who coined the term Internet of Things?**

    a. Vint Cerf

    b. Kevin Ashton

    c. Tim Berners-Lee

    d. Marc Andreessen

86. **In what year was the term Internet of Things coined?**

    a. 1995

    b. 1999

    c. 2003

    d. 2007

87. **What is an IoT network?**

    a. A collection of networked devices

    b. A collection of interconnected devices

    c. A collection of signaled devices

    d. None of the above

88. **Which technology is most closely associated with the foundation of IoT?**

    a. Bluetooth

    b. RFID

    c. GPS

    d. Wi-Fi

89. **What do API systems enable?**

    a. Network service portability is allowed by API

    b. Systems service portability is allowed by API

    c. Device service portability is allowed by API

    d. All of these

90. **Why is the scalability of IoT systems a challenge?**
    a. Limited number of devices
    b. High cost of scaling
    c. Integration with existing systems
    d. Uniform network protocols

91. **What challenge is associated with the varying lifecycles of IoT devices?**
    a. Device interoperability
    b. Data encryption
    c. Device management
    d. Data analysis

92. **Why is firmware updating a challenge in IoT?**
    a. It requires constant internet access
    b. Devices often have limited processing power
    c. Devices have extensive storage
    d. Firmware updates are rare

93. **Which of the following is a challenge related to IoT data analysis?**
    a. Low data generation
    b. Limited analytical tools
    c. Processing large volumes of data
    d. Lack of data visualization

94. **What is a challenge of ensuring real-time data processing in IoT?**
    a. High storage capacity
    b. Low data transfer rates
    c. High latency
    d. Uniform data formats

95. **Which aspect of IoT poses a challenge due to limited device computational resources?**
    a. Strong encryption
    b. Frequent software updates
    c. Complex data processing
    d. Seamless integration

96. **What is a significant challenge in managing the heterogeneity of IoT devices?**
    a. Data uniformity
    b. Device calibration
    c. Device standardization
    d. Device fragmentation

97. **Which challenge involves the need for reliable and efficient IoT device authentication?**
    a. Device redundancy
    b. Device interoperability
    c. Device security
    d. Device calibration

98. **What challenge arises due to the deployment of IoT devices in harsh environments?**
    a. High energy consumption
    b. Physical durability
    c. Data redundancy
    d. Over-the-air updates

99. **Which challenge is associated with the energy efficiency of IoT devices?**
    a. Excessive power consumption
    b. Unlimited battery life
    c. Over-the-air power supply
    d. Minimal energy use

100. **Why is data governance a challenge in IoT?**
    a. Data encryption issues
    b. Undefined data ownership
    c. Data minimization
    d. Data uniformity

101. **Which challenge involves ensuring the reliability of data from IoT devices?**
    a. Data encryption
    b. Data redundancy
    c. Data accuracy
    d. Data deletion

102. **Which organization is responsible for the development of the MQTT protocol?**

    a. IEEE

    b. OASIS

    c. W3C

    d. IETF

103. **What does the acronym CoAP stand for in the context of IoT?**

    a. Communication Access Protocol

    b. Constrained Application Protocol

    c. Connected Application Protocol

    d. Cooperative Access Protocol

104. **Which standard is commonly used for wireless communication in smart home devices?**

    a. Zigbee

    b. FTP

    c. SMTP

    d. POP3

105. **Which organization developed the IEEE 802.15.4 standard?**

    a. ISO

    b. ITU

    c. IEEE

    d. W3C

106. **What is the main purpose of the LoRaWAN protocol in IoT?**

    a. High-speed data transfer

    b. Long-range communication

    c. Real-time data processing

    d. Secure data encryption

107. **Which IoT standard is specifically designed for low-power wide-area networks (LPWAN)?**

    a. Wi-Fi

    b. Bluetooth

    c. LoRaWAN

    d. Zigbee

108. **What does the acronym NB-IoT stand for?**

    a. Narrowband Internet of Things

    b. Network-based Internet of Things

    c. New broadband Internet of Things

    d. Node-based Internet of Things

109. **Which standard is used for short-range wireless communication between IoT devices and smartphones?**

    a. Zigbee

    b. Wi-Fi

    c. Bluetooth

    d. LoRaWAN

110. **Which protocol is widely used for remote device management in IoT?**

    a. HTTP

    b. SNMP

    c. CoAP

    d. MQTT

111. **Which IoT connectivity standard operates in the industrial, scientific, and medical (ISM) radio band?**

    a. Zigbee

    b. Ethernet

    c. LTE

    d. 5G

112. **What is the primary function of the 6LoWPAN standard in IoT?**

    a. High-speed data transfer

    b. Low-power wireless personal area networking

    c. Secure data encryption

    d. Real-time data processing

113. **Which organization is responsible for developing the Z-Wave standard for smart home devices?**

    a. IEEE

    b. ITU

    c. Z-Wave Alliance

    d. W3C

114. **What does the acronym AMQP stand for in IoT?**

    a. Asynchronous Messaging Queue Protocol

    b. Advanced Message Queuing Protocol

    c. Application Management Queue Protocol

    d. Automated Messaging Queue Protocol

115. **Which standard is designed for short-range communication and is used in IoT for device-to-device interaction?**

    a. Bluetooth Low Energy (BLE)

    b. Wi-Fi Direct

    c. Ethernet

    d. Zigbee

116. **Which IoT protocol operates on the principle of publish-subscribe messaging?**

    a. HTTP

    b. CoAP

    c. MQTT

    d. SNMP

117. **What is the primary use of the OPC UA standard in IoT?**

    a. Real-time data processing

    b. Secure data transmission

    c. Interoperability in industrial automation

    d. Long-range communication

118. **Which IoT standard is known for its ultra-narrowband technology suitable for long-range communication?**

    a. Zigbee

    b. Sigfox

    c. Wi-Fi

    d. Bluetooth

119. **What does the acronym DDS stand for in the context of IoT communication?**

    a. Data Delivery Service

    b. Data Distribution Service

    c. Device Data Service

    d. Distributed Device Service

120. **Which protocol is used for resource-constrained devices in IoT to communicate over the internet?**

    a. FTP

    b. CoAP

    c. SMTP

    d. IMAP

121. **Which wireless technology is most suitable for low-power, short-range communication in IoT?**

    a. Wi-Fi

    b. Bluetooth

    c. 4G LTE

    d. Ethernet

122. **What is the primary advantage of using 5G technology in IoT?**

    a. Low bandwidth

    b. High latency

    c. High data transfer speed

    d. Short-range communication

123. **Which of the following is a major benefit of using LPWAN in IoT?**

    a. High power consumption

    b. Short-range communication

    c. Long battery life

    d. High data transfer speed

124. **Which type of network topology is commonly used in IoT to connect multiple devices?**

    a. Star

    b. Ring

    c. Bus

    d. Mesh

125. **What is a key feature of the Zigbee connectivity standard in IoT?**

    a. High data transfer rates

    b. Low power consumption

    c. Long-range communication

    d. High bandwidth

126. **What is the primary function of a gateway in IoT connectivity?**
    a. To provide power to devices
    b. To connect IoT devices to the internet
    c. To encrypt data
    d. To store data locally

127. **What is the advantage of using Ethernet in IoT connectivity?**
    a. Wireless communication
    b. High reliability and stability
    c. Low installation cost
    d. Long-range communication

128. **Which IoT connectivity technology is best suited for devices requiring low data rates and long battery life?**
    a. Wi-Fi
    b. LTE
    c. Zigbee
    d. Ethernet

129. **What does the acronym LPWAN stand for in the context of IoT connectivity?**
    a. Low power wireless area network
    b. Long power wide area network
    c. Low-power wide-area network
    d. Long performance wireless area network

130. **Which IoT connectivity technology is characterized by ultra-low power consumption and long-range communication?**
    a. Wi-Fi
    b. Zigbee
    c. LoRa
    d. Bluetooth

131. **Which of the following is not an application of IoT?**
    a. Smart homes
    b. Wearable devices
    c. Social media
    d. Industrial automation

132. **In a smart home, which device is commonly controlled by IoT technology?**

    a. Television

    b. Washing machine

    c. Lights

    d. Blender

133. **Which IoT application involves the use of sensors to monitor soil moisture levels?**

    a. Smart city

    b. Smart agriculture

    c. Smart healthcare

    d. Smart retail

134. **What type of network is typically used to connect IoT devices?**

    a. Wi-Fi

    b. LAN

    c. WAN

    d. MAN

135. **Which of the following is a key feature of IoT?**

    a. Manual operation

    b. Connectivity

    c. Standalone devices

    d. Offline data processing

136. **In smart cities, IoT can be used for:**

    a. Waste management

    b. Traffic control

    c. Energy management

    d. All of the above

137. **Which of the following is an example of a wearable IoT device?**

    a. Smart watch

    b. Smart refrigerator

    c. Smart thermostat

    d. Smart light

138. Which of the following is a cloud service provider for IoT?

    a. AWS IoT

    b. Google Maps

    c. Facebook

    d. Instagram

139. What type of data do smart meters in IoT collect?

    a. Temperature

    b. Energy consumption

    c. Humidity

    d. Air quality

140. Which IoT application can help reduce energy consumption in buildings?

    a. Smart thermostats

    b. Smart TVs

    c. Smart locks

    d. Smart cameras

141. In the context of IoT, what does the term actuator mean?

    a. A device that detects changes

    b. A device that performs actions

    c. A device that stores data

    d. A device that analyzes data

142. Which IoT application can be used to monitor air quality in a city?

    a. Smart homes

    b. Smart healthcare

    c. Smart environment

    d. Smart retail

143. Which of the following is a common IoT communication protocol?

    a. HTTPS

    b. UDP

    c. CoAP

    d. POP3

144. **What is the primary purpose of IoT in transportation?**

    a. Enhance driving experience

    b. Monitor and manage traffic

    c. Provide entertainment

    d. Facilitate social interaction

145. **Which IoT application is used in logistics for tracking goods?**

    a. Smart home

    b. Smart logistics

    c. Smart healthcare

    d. Smart retail

146. **Which IoT device is used for home security?**

    a. Smart lock

    b. Smart fridge

    c. Smart oven

    d. Smart washing machine

147. **In IoT, what is a smart grid?**

    a. An intelligent electricity distribution network

    b. A grid for smart devices

    c. A social media network

    d. An internet service provider

148. **Which technology is often used for location tracking in IoT?**

    a. GPS

    b. Wi-Fi

    c. Bluetooth

    d. RFID

149. **What type of data is collected by environmental sensors in IoT?**

    a. Air quality

    b. Traffic patterns

    c. User preferences

    d. Social media trends

150. **Which of the following is an IoT device for health monitoring?**

    a. Smart thermostat

    b. Smart watch

    c. Smart light

    d. Smart fridge

151. **What does Zigbee technology offer in IoT applications?**

    a. High bandwidth

    b. Local connectivity with low power consumption

    c. High speed

    d. Long range

152. **Which IoT service helps in predictive maintenance of industrial equipment?**

    a. Smart retail

    b. Smart healthcare

    c. Smart manufacturing

    d. Smart agriculture

153. **Which IoT application involves the use of connected devices to control and automate home functions?**

    a. Smart retail

    b. Smart home

    c. Smart health

    d. Smart logistics

154. **In the context of IoT, what is a digital twin?**

    a. A virtual representation of a physical object

    b. A physical clone of a device

    c. A duplicate network

    d. A pair of sensors

155. **What is the primary advantage of using IoT in agriculture?**

    a. Enhanced entertainment

    b. Improved crop management

    c. Increased social connectivity

    d. Better indoor climate control

156. **Which of the following is a common application of IoT in the retail industry?**

    a. Smart shelves

    b. Smart locks

    c. Smart meters

    d. Smart watches

157. **Which IoT device can be used to automate lighting in a home?**

    a. Smart bulb

    b. Smart fridge

    c. Smart TV

    d. Smart washing machine

158. **What is the role of data analytics in IoT?**

    a. Data collection

    b. Data analysis and insights

    c. Data storage

    d. Data transmission

159. **Which of the following is a key challenge in IoT implementation?**

    a. Device design

    b. Data security

    c. Device color

    d. Device size

160. **In IoT, what is meant by interoperability?**

    a. Devices from different vendors working together

    b. Devices with the same design

    c. Devices with high power consumption

    d. Devices with the same operating system

161. **Which IoT application can help cities manage their resources more efficiently?**

    a. Smart home

    b. Smart city

    c. Smart health

    d. Smart retail

162. What does the term machine-to-machine communication refer to in IoT?

a. Direct communication between devices

b. Human to device communication

c. Device to cloud communication

d. Human-to-human communication

163. Which technology is used in IoT for real-time data collection and analysis?

a. Edge computing

b. Batch processing

c. Offline processing

d. Manual processing

164. Which IoT application can enhance the shopping experience for customers?

a. Smart manufacturing

b. Smart retail

c. Smart agriculture

d. Smart health

165. What is the main goal of IoT in healthcare?

a. Improve patient care

b. Enhance social media presence

c. Increase entertainment options

d. Improve office productivity

166. In IoT, what does the term cloud computing refer to?

a. Storing and accessing data over the internet

b. Manual data processing

c. Local data storage

d. Offline data processing

167. Which of the following is an example of an IoT device in the automotive industry?

a. Smart thermostat

b. Smart light

c. Connected car

d. Smart fridge

168. **What is the main benefit of using IoT in logistics?**

    a. Real-time tracking and monitoring

    b. Increased entertainment options

    c. Improved office productivity

    d. Enhanced social connectivity

169. **Which IoT application involves using connected devices to monitor and manage the health of livestock?**

    a. Smart agriculture

    b. Smart health

    c. Smart home

    d. Smart retail

Join our Discord space

Join our Discord workspace for latest updates, offers, tech happenings around the world, new releases, and sessions with the authors:

https://discord.bpbonline.com

Answers

Q.No.	Answers	Q.No.	Answers	Q.No.	Answers	Q.No.	Answers	Q.No.	Answers
1	b	31	b	61	b	91	c	121	b
2	c	32	d	62	b	92	b	122	c
3	b	33	c	63	d	93	c	123	c
4	b	34	b	64	c	94	c	124	d
5	c	35	c	65	b	95	c	125	b
6	c	36	c	66	c	96	d	126	b
7	c	37	b	67	a	97	c	127	b
8	c	38	c	68	c	98	b	128	c
9	c	39	b	69	b	99	a	129	c
10	b	40	a	70	b	100	b	130	c
11	c	41	d	71	b	101	c	131	c
12	c	42	b	72	b	102	b	132	c
13	b	43	d	73	c	103	b	133	b
14	c	44	b	74	c	104	a	134	a
15	b	45	a	75	b	105	c	135	b
16	d	46	b	76	c	106	b	136	d
17	c	47	c	77	b	107	c	137	a
18	a	48	a	78	b	108	a	138	a
19	a	49	a	79	c	109	c	139	b
20	b	50	b	80	a	110	b	140	a
21	c	51	c	81	b	111	a	141	b
22	b	52	b	82	c	112	b	142	c
23	c	53	b	83	b	113	c	143	c
24	c	54	c	84	b	114	b	144	b
25	c	55	c	85	b	115	a	145	b
26	c	56	c	86	b	116	c	146	a
27	d	57	d	87	c	117	c	147	a
28	b	58	c	88	b	118	b	148	a
29	b	59	b	89	d	119	b	149	a
30	d	60	c	90	c	120	b	150	b

Q.No.	Answers	Q.No.	Answers
151	b	161	b
152	c	162	a
153	b	163	a
154	a	164	b
155	b	165	a
156	a	166	a
157	a	167	c
158	b	168	a
159	b	169	a
160	a		

Join our Discord space

Join our Discord workspace for latest updates, offers, tech happenings around the world, new releases, and sessions with the authors:

https://discord.bpbonline.com

CHAPTER 2
Building Blocks of IoT

Introduction

The impact of the IoT on businesses, households, and metropolitan areas has increased dramatically during the last decade. Although IoT is a word that is often used in tech conversations, these systems' true power and creativity lie in their foundational components. Collectively, these components provide the groundwork for turning everyday items into intelligent, networked gadgets. Let us take a closer look at these crucial parts:

- **First, actuators and sensors**: Sensing is the lifeblood of every Internet of Things gadget. Sensors that monitor things like temperature, humidity, motion, and light level make this possible. Some sensors are even sensitive enough to detect chemicals or track heart rates. Actuators are then used to make a change in the physical environment in response to the data that has been perceived. For instance, if the temperature in a room increases over a specific threshold, an actuator may activate a fan.

- **Two-way communication**: Sending the sensor data to other devices or a centralized system for analysis is essential for the data to be valuable. Connectivity has a role here. Wi-Fi, cellular, Bluetooth, Zigbee, and **low-power wide-area networks (LPWAN)** are only a few possible network connections for a given scenario and infrastructure.

- **Processing of information**: It is necessary to process data once it has been gathered and transferred. Edge computing and fog computing are two types of local processing, while cloud computing is another. The time urgency involved and the amount of information usually determine the best option. Real-time activities, such as autonomous driving, need processing at the edge (i.e., inside the automobile itself). Cloud processing, on the other hand, is often used for less time-sensitive data, such as daily weather forecasts.

- **Data archiving**: The massive volume of data produced by IoT devices necessitates using reliable and easily accessible storage methods. This is because of its scalability and convenience, cloud-based storage solutions are quickly becoming the norm. However, hybrid storage systems combining local and cloud storage may be the best option when data sensitivity, restrictions, and retrieval demands are taken into account.

- **User interface (UI)**: Following the completion of data analysis, the results should be made available to the target audience. This might be accomplished via various means, including mobile applications, online portals, and other devices. The data may be explored, orders issued, or choices made using this user interface. For example, health data collected by a fitness tracker may be shown graphically via a smartphone app.

- **Analytical methods and synthetic intelligence (AI)**: While the observation of raw data might provide practical conclusions, the true potential of the Internet of Things resides in using this data for predictive modeling, decision automation, and pattern recognition. Algorithms based on artificial intelligence and advanced analytics can sift through massive amounts of data to provide valuable insights, power automation, and make predictions.

- **Safety and security**: Security is a crucial component of the Internet of Things due to the potentially disastrous consequences of a breach (see smart cities or industrial IoT) and the potentially personal and sensitive nature of some of the data gathered. This involves protecting data at rest and in transit and ensuring the hardware can withstand assaults.

- **Integrating and standardizing**: The proliferation of IoT device makers underscores the need for standardized protocols to facilitate efficient and effective interoperability.

Multiple choice questions

1. **What are the fundamental building blocks of the IoT?**

    a. Servers and routers

    b. Sensors, connectivity, data processing, and user interface

    c. Virtual reality and artificial intelligence

    d. Cloud computing and blockchain

2. **Which component of IoT is responsible for collecting data from the environment?**

    a. Sensors

    b. Servers

    c. Databases

    d. User interfaces

3. **Which building block of IoT is responsible for processing and analyzing the collected data?**

    a. Sensors

    b. User interfaces

    c. Data processing

    d. Connectivity

4. **What role does cloud computing play in the IoT ecosystem?**

    a. Cloud computing is not related to IoT

    b. It provides a way to store IoT devices physically

    c. It offers data storage, processing, and analysis capabilities

    d. It connects IoT devices using Bluetooth

5. **Which of the following is not a type of IoT communication model?**

    a. Point-to-point

    b. Star

    c. Mesh

    d. Linear

6. **What is the purpose of a digital twin in an IoT system?**

    a. It represents a physical location for IoT devices

    b. It provides a visual interface for users to interact with IoT data

    c. It is a virtual replica of a physical IoT device or system

    d. It generates energy for IoT devices

7. **Which protocol type is typically used for long-range communication in cellular IoT networks?**

    a. Wi-Fi

    b. Bluetooth

    c. 5G

    d. Zigbee

8. **Which layer of the IoT architecture deals with user interfaces and applications?**

    a. Perception layer

    b. Network layer

    c. Application layer

    d. Data layer

9. **What is the role of middleware in IoT systems?**

    a. It controls the physical devices in IoT networks

    b. It stores data generated by IoT devices

    c. It provides communication between applications and devices

    d. It generates power for IoT devices

10. **What does the term sensor fusion refer to in IoT?**

    a. Combining multiple sensors' data to improve accuracy and reliability

    b. Creating virtual sensors for IoT simulations

    c. Using sensors to create a fusion energy source

    d. Developing sensors with advanced user interfaces

11. **Which key concept in IoT enables devices to not only sense the environment but also to take autonomous actions based on real-time analysis?**

    a. Actuator programming

    b. Edge analytics

    c. Fog computing

    d. Device virtualization

12. **What is the purpose of a network protocol in IoT?**

    a. To secure physical devices

    b. To ensure data privacy

    c. To facilitate communication between devices

    d. To provide power to devices

13. **What is the primary advantage of using IPv6 in IoT networks?**

    a. It is easier to set up than IPv4

    b. It provides backward compatibility with older devices

    c. It offers a larger address space to accommodate more devices

    d. It requires less power for communication

14. **What are the fundamental components of an IoT system?**

    a. IoT framework

    b. IoT architecture

    c. IoT network

    d. IoT ecosystem

15. **Which layer of the IoT architecture deals with physical devices and sensors?**

    a. Application layer

    b. Network layer

    c. Perception layer

    d. Data layer

16. **Which of the following algorithms would be the best choice for optimizing routing in an IoT network where power consumption is a critical factor?**

    a. Open shortest path first (OSPF)

    b. Ad hoc on-demand distance vector (AODV)

    c. Routing information protocol (RIP)

    d. Low energy adaptive clustering hierarchy (LEACH)

17. **Which of the following is not a typical communication pattern in IoT?**

    a. Device-to-device (D2D)

    b. Device-to-cloud (D2C)

    c. Cloud-to-cloud (C2C)

    d. Device-to-user (D2U)

18. **Which layer of the IoT architecture is responsible for data storage, processing, and analysis?**

    a. Application layer

    b. Network layer

    c. Data layer

    d. Perception layer

19. **In IoT, which of the following technologies is most suited for enabling smart cities by providing low-cost, high-efficiency power management?**

    a. Near Field Communication (NFC)

    b. LPWAN

    c. Virtual private networks (VPN)

    d. Data distribution service (DDS)

20. **Which of the following is a key challenge in IoT security?**

    a. Insufficient data collection

    b. Limited device compatibility

    c. Lack of network coverage

    d. Data privacy and authentication

21. **Which of the following describes the function of a digital twin in IoT systems?**

    a. A software simulation of an IoT device's firmware

    b. A cloud service that aggregates and processes sensor data

    c. A virtual replica of a physical object used for real-time data analysis and decision making

    d. A redundancy mechanism for fault tolerance in IoT networks

22. **Which of the following is not a type of IoT connectivity protocol?**

    a. HTTP

    b. CoAP

    c. MQTT

    d. JTAG

23. **What is the primary role of the application layer in the IoT architecture?**

    a. Managing device connectivity

    b. Handling data storage and analysis

    c. Processing raw sensor data

    d. Providing user interfaces and services

24. **Which of the following is a critical consideration for IoT device design?**

    a. Maximizing power consumption for longer device life

    b. Prioritizing data security over connectivity

    c. Increasing device complexity for enhanced functionality

    d. Balancing power efficiency and performance

25. **Which layer of the IoT architecture manages device discovery and addressing?**

    a. Perception layer

    b. Network layer

    c. Application layer

    d. Data layer

26. **What is the purpose of an IoT protocol like Constrained Application Protocol (CoAP)?**
    a. Transmitting large data files between devices
    b. Ensuring compatibility between different IoT platforms
    c. Enabling communication between resource-constrained devices and servers
    d. Enhancing data security in IoT networks

27. **Which of the following IoT deployment models involves direct communication between devices within a local range?**
    a. Cloud-based IoT
    b. Fog/Edge-based IoT
    c. Hybrid IoT
    d. Device-to-device (D2D) IoT

28. **What is the primary role of the data layer in the IoT architecture?**
    a. Managing device hardware and firmware
    b. Handling device communication protocols
    c. Storing and processing data generated by devices
    d. Providing user interfaces for device control

29. **Which of the following is not a layer in the traditional IoT architecture model?**
    a. Application layer
    b. Cloud layer
    c. Network layer
    d. Data layer

30. **What is the purpose of a sensor in an IoT device?**
    a. Initiate physical actions
    b. Process and analyze data
    c. Collect data from the environment
    d. Store historical data

31. **What is the main benefit of using MQTT for IoT communication?**
    a. High data transfer rates
    b. Real-time data analysis
    c. Low power consumption
    d. Reliable communication over unreliable networks

32. **Which type of device serves as an intermediary between IoT devices and the cloud?**
    a. Sensor
    b. Actuator
    c. Gateway
    d. RFID tag

33. **Which of the following is an example of a short-range wireless communication technology used in IoT?**
    a. Wi-Fi
    b. LoRaWAN
    c. 4G
    d. Satellite communication

34. **What is the primary purpose of a digital dashboard in an IoT system?**
    a. Secure data storage
    b. Real-time data visualization and monitoring,
    c. Data analysis and processing
    d. Device configuration and firmware updates

35. **Which of the following is not a common application area for IoT technology?**
    a. Healthcare
    b. Agriculture
    c. Astrophysics
    d. Smart cities

36. **Which IoT communication protocol is known for its low-power consumption and suitability for battery-operated devices?**
    a. HTTP
    b. Zigbee
    c. MQTT
    d. TCP/IP

37. **What is the purpose of a digital sensor in an IoT device?**
    a. Transmitting data to the cloud
    b. Initiating physical actions
    c. Processing data
    d. Collecting and converting environmental data into digital signals

38. **What does the term fog computing refer to in IoT architecture?**

    a. Data processing and analysis at the cloud server

    b. Data storage on the IoT device

    c. Data processing and analysis at the edge/gateway devices

    d. Data transmission between cloud servers

39. **What is the purpose of a microcontroller in an IoT device?**

    a. Transmitting data to the cloud

    b. Collecting and converting sensor data

    c. Providing network connectivity

    d. Initiating physical actions

40. **Which IoT connectivity technology is designed for short-range, low-power communication between devices within a few meters?**

    a. Zigbee

    b. LoRaWAN

    c. 5G

    d. Wi-Fi

41. **What is the role of a protocol in IoT communication?**

    a. It serves as a physical connector between devices

    b. It defines the rules and format for data exchange between devices

    c. It powers the actuators in IoT devices

    d. It generates visual representations of data

42. **Which layer of the IoT architecture handles user interfaces, applications, and services?**

    a. Application layer

    b. Data layer

    c. Perception layer

    d. Network layer

43. **What is the primary purpose of a cloud service in IoT?**

    a. Collecting sensor data

    b. Storing data on the device

    c. Analyzing data locally

    d. Storing and processing data remotely

44. Which of the following is a common challenge in IoT device management?

    a. Insufficient data generation

    b. Incompatibility between protocols

    c. Lack of data security measures

    d. Reliability of wireless communication

45. Which type of network topology is often used in IoT systems for device-to-device communication?

    a. Bus

    b. Star

    c. Mesh

    d. Ring

46. What is the primary goal of edge computing in the context of IoT?

    a. To process data on the cloud server

    b. To reduce data transmission costs

    c. To minimize the use of sensors

    d. To process data locally on the IoT device or gateway

47. What does the acronym REST mean in IoT communication?

    a. Reliable Energy Storage Technology

    b. Robust Encryption and Security Technique

    c. Representational State Transfer

    d. Responsive Environment Sensing Technology

48. What is the primary function of an IoT platform?

    a. Transmitting data to the cloud

    b. Data visualization

    c. Remote device control

    d. Enabling device management and application development

49. Which IoT deployment model involves centralizing data processing and analysis at the cloud server?

    a. Edge computing

    b. Cloud-based IoT

    c. Fog computing

    d. Hybrid IoT

50. **What is the purpose of a unique identifier like a MAC address in an IoT device?**
    a. To provide device authentication
    b. To determine device location
    c. To enable real-time data analysis
    d. To initiate physical actions

51. **Which communication model involves communication between the cloud and devices without direct device-to-device interaction?**
    a. Device-to-device (D2D) communication
    b. Device-to-cloud (D2C) communication
    c. Device-to-gateway (D2G) communication
    d. Peer-to-peer (P2P) communication

52. **What is the role of a protocol converter in an IoT system?**
    a. Translating data between different communication protocols
    b. Generating sensor data
    c. Providing power to the IoT devices
    d. Storing historical data

53. **Which of the following communication protocols is known for its lightweight and low-power characteristics, making it suitable for IoT devices?**
    a. TCP/IP
    b. HTTP
    c. CoAP
    d. SMTP

54. **Which layer of the IoT architecture handles data routing and forwarding among devices?**
    a. Perception layer
    b. Application layer
    c. Network layer
    d. Data layer

55. **What is the purpose of device provisioning in IoT?**
    a. Creating physical replicas of IoT devices
    b. Managing user interfaces on IoT devices
    c. Enabling secure onboarding of devices to the network
    d. Processing and analyzing data on IoT devices

56. **Which of the following is a key consideration for managing IoT device power consumption?**

    a. Increasing data transmission frequency

    b. Using high-power processors

    c. Optimizing data transfer rates

    d. Maximizing battery life

57. **What does the term mesh networking refer to in the context of IoT communication?**

    a. Direct device-to-device communication without gateways

    b. Communication between devices and the cloud only

    c. Communication through a central server

    d. Communication using short-range wireless technology

58. **What is the primary function of a digital identity in the IoT ecosystem?**

    a. Providing entertainment services to users

    b. Establishing a device's reputation online

    c. Authenticating devices and enabling secure communication

    d. Generating random data for security purposes

59. **Which of the following is a challenge associated with IoT data management?**

    a. Excessive data storage

    b. Data security and privacy concerns

    c. Limited device compatibility

    d. Lack of network coverage

60. **Which communication model involves data exchange between devices within a local range without involving the cloud or a central server?**

    a. Device-to-cloud (D2C) communication

    b. Cloud-to-device (C2D) communication

    c. Device-to-device (D2D) communication

    d. Device-to-gateway (D2G) communication

61. **Which of the following is not a consideration when selecting wireless communication technology for an IoT application?**

    a. Data transfer speed

    b. Power consumption

    c. Security capabilities

    d. Number of available IoT platforms

62. **In the context of IoT, what does over-the-air (OTA) refer to?**
    a. Communication between devices using satellite links
    b. Communication between devices using Ethernet cables
    c. Remote firmware updates and configuration changes for devices
    d. Data transfer using USB cables

63. **Which of the following is not a benefit of using edge computing in IoT systems?**
    a. Reduced latency
    b. Lower data transmission costs
    c. Enhanced data security
    d. Centralized data processing

64. **What is the purpose of device management in the context of IoT?**
    a. Providing entertainment services to users
    b. Enabling secure data transmission
    c. Ensuring the proper functioning of devices throughout their lifecycle
    d. Analyzing and processing data on the cloud server

65. **Which of the following is not a primary communication technology used in IoT networks?**
    a. Bluetooth
    b. Ethernet
    c. Wi-Fi
    d. SMS

66. **Which wireless technologies are typically used for short-range communication between devices like smartphones and wearables?**
    a. Zigbee
    b. Bluetooth
    c. LoRaWAN
    d. LTE

67. **Which type of IoT communication involves device and user interaction through interfaces like mobile apps or web dashboards?**
    a. Device-to-device (D2D) communication
    b. Device-to-cloud (D2C) communication
    c. Device-to-user (D2U) communication
    d. Peer-to-peer (P2P) communication

68. **Which of the following is a key challenge in IoT device security?**

    a. Insufficient data storage capacity

    b. Limited network coverage

    c. Incompatibility between protocols

    d. Vulnerability to cyberattacks

69. **In the context of IoT security, what does end-to-end encryption mean?**

    a. Encrypting data at rest on devices

    b. Encrypting data during transmission between devices and the cloud

    c. Encrypting data within a device's memory

    d. Encrypting data only in the cloud server

70. **What is the purpose of a digital signature in IoT communication?**

    a. To indicate the manufacturer of the device

    b. To add decorative elements to data packets

    c. To authenticate the origin and integrity of data

    d. To generate random data for security purposes

71. **Which of the following is a common challenge in IoT data management?**

    a. Limited data generation

    b. Slow data transfer rates

    c. Insufficient data storage

    d. Lack of data analytics platforms

72. **What is the primary purpose of data fusion in IoT systems?**

    a. Enhancing device connectivity

    b. Ensuring data security

    c. Combining and processing data from multiple sources

    d. Generating random data for testing purposes

73. **What is the role of a security framework in the context of IoT?**

    a. Providing a physical enclosure for IoT devices

    b. Ensuring device compatibility with different networks

    c. Implementing encryption algorithms for data security

    d. Managing user interfaces for IoT devices

74. **Which IoT architecture layer manages device communication, addressing, and routing?**

    a. Application layer

    b. Perception layer

    c. Network layer

    d. Data layer

75. **Which of the following is a benefit of using fog computing in IoT systems?**

    a. Centralized data processing on cloud servers

    b. Reduced latency for data transmission

    c. Decreased need for sensor devices

    d. Lower power consumption in devices

76. **What does the term edge device refer to in the context of IoT architecture?**

    a. A device located at the center of a network topology

    b. A device that connects directly to the cloud server

    c. A device that processes data at the network's edge, near the data source

    d. A device with high computational power used for data analysis

77. **What is the main advantage of using IPv6 for IoT networks compared to IPv4?**

    a. Smaller address space

    b. Limited device compatibility

    c. Larger address space

    d. Faster data transmission

78. **What is the primary purpose of a sensor node in IoT networks?**

    a. Data processing and analysis

    b. Data storage in the cloud

    c. Collecting and transmitting sensor data

    d. Initiating physical actions

79. **In IoT, what does latency refer to?**

    a. The time taken for data to travel between devices and the cloud

    b. The time taken to process data on IoT devices

    c. The energy consumption of IoT devices

    d. The speed of data transmission between devices

80. Which of the following is a common challenge in IoT device connectivity?

    a. Low data transmission rates

    b. Incompatible device form factors

    c. Lack of data analytics platforms

    d. Insufficient energy efficiency

81. What is the purpose of a system on a chip (SoC) in IoT devices?

    a. Providing power to the device

    b. Initiating physical actions

    c. Enabling communication with the cloud

    d. Integrating multiple components onto a single chip

82. Which IoT architecture layer manages data storage, processing, and analysis?

    a. Network layer

    b. Perception layer

    c. Application layer

    d. Data layer

83. What is the role of cloudlets in fog computing architecture?

    a. Processing data on the cloud server

    b. Storing data locally on IoT devices

    c. Providing communication between devices and the cloud,

    d. Processing data at the edge of the network, closer to the data source

84. Which type of device management involves remotely updating the firmware and software of the IoT devices?

    a. Device provisioning

    b. Device authentication

    c. Device configuration

    d. Over-the-air (OTA) updates

85. What does the term wearable IoT refer to?

    a. IoT devices with built-in clothing sensors

    b. IoT devices that can be worn by users

    c. IoT devices for pets and animals

    d. IoT devices for industrial applications

86. **Which of the following is a key consideration for selecting IoT communication protocols?**
    a. High data transfer rates
    b. Complexity of protocol
    c. Number of available devices
    d. Number of IoT platforms

87. **What is the purpose of protocol standardization in IoT?**
    a. Limiting the number of devices in an IoT network
    b. Ensuring device compatibility with different networks
    c. Providing power to the devices
    d. Defining uniform communication rules for devices

88. **Which layer of the IoT architecture manages the interaction between devices and users or applications?**
    a. Data layer
    b. Perception layer
    c. Network layer
    d. Application layer

89. **What is the main purpose of device authentication in IoT security?**
    a. Providing energy to IoT devices
    b. Ensuring device compatibility with different networks
    c. Establishing secure communication between devices and users
    d. Identifying and verifying the identity of devices in a network

90. **When dealing with constrained IoT devices, what is a major challenge in using traditional public-key cryptography methods for securing communication?**
    a. Limited network bandwidth
    b. High computational requirements
    c. Lack of cloud integration
    d. Inability to support 5G networks

91. **In the context of IoT security, what is identity and access management (IAM)?**
    a. The process of managing device compatibility
    b. Ensuring the availability of IoT devices
    c. Managing user identities and their access to devices and data
    d. Processing and analyzing IoT data

92. Which wireless technology is suitable for IoT applications that require high data transfer rates and low latency, such as autonomous vehicles?

a. LoRaWAN

b. 5G

c. Zigbee

d. NFC

93. What does the term edge analytics refer to in IoT systems?

a. Analyzing data on the cloud server

b. Analyzing data on the IoT device itself

c. Analyzing data on a gateway or edge device

d. Analyzing data at a central data center

94. Which IoT architecture layer focuses on the physical components and sensors that collect data from the environment?

a. Network layer

b. Data layer

c. Perception layer

d. Application layer

95. What is the role of a broker in MQTT communication?

a. Initiating data transmission between devices

b. Storing data on the cloud server

c. Managing user identities and access

d. Facilitating communication between publisher and subscriber devices

96. What does data aggregation refer to in the context of IoT data management?

a. Processing data on the cloud server

b. Combining and summarizing data from multiple sources

c. Storing data in a centralized location

d. Generating random data for testing purposes

97. Which IoT deployment model combines cloud computing and edge computing for data processing and analysis?

a. Fog computing

b. Cloud-based IoT

c. Hybrid IoT

d. Device-to-device (D2D) IoT

98. **What is the primary purpose of anomaly detection in IoT systems?**

    a. Initiating physical actions based on sensor data

    b. Storing historical data

    c. Identifying unusual or abnormal behavior in data

    d. Processing and analyzing data in real time

99. **In the context of IoT security, what is the purpose of access control?**

    a. Providing power to the devices

    b. Managing user identities and their access to devices and data

    c. Processing and analyzing IoT data

    d. Establishing secure communication between devices

100. **Which of the following is a consideration for ensuring data privacy in IoT systems?**

    a. Maximizing data transmission rates

    b. Transmitting data without encryption

    c. Storing data in publicly accessible locations

    d. Encrypting sensitive data during transmission and storage

101. **What is the primary function of a software-defined sensor in IoT devices?**

    a. Initiating physical actions

    b. Collecting data from the environment

    c. Storing historical data

    d. Providing power to the device

102. **What is the role of a firewall in IoT security?**

    a. Initiating physical actions in case of security breaches

    b. Processing and analyzing IoT data

    c. Filtering and monitoring network traffic to prevent unauthorized access

    d. Generating random data for testing purposes

103. **Which IoT architecture layer manages data storage and retrieval for long-term analysis and reporting?**

    a. Data layer

    b. Network layer

    c. Application layer

    d. Perception layer

104. What does digital footprint refer to in IoT security?

    a. The physical size of IoT devices

    b. The energy consumption of IoT devices

    c. A device's presence and activities on the internet

    d. The number of sensors in an IoT device

105. In the context of IoT communication, what is a payload?

    a. The physical size of an IoT device

    b. The energy consumption of an IoT device

    c. The data being transmitted between devices

    d. The geographic location of an IoT device

106. What is the primary function of a device driver in IoT systems?

    a. Storing historical data

    b. Initiating physical actions

    c. Enabling communication between devices and applications

    d. Processing and analyzing data

107. What is the purpose of a system integrator in IoT projects?

    a. Collecting and storing sensor data

    b. Providing power to the devices

    c. Managing device authentication

    d. Combining various hardware and software components into a functional system

108. What is the primary function of a supervisory control and data acquisition (SCADA) system in IoT applications?

    a. Processing data on the cloud server

    b. Initiating physical actions

    c. Monitoring and controlling industrial processes remotely

    d. Storing historical data

109. In IoT communication, what is the purpose of a communication protocol?

    a. Managing device hardware and firmware

    b. Defining the rules and format for data exchange between devices,

    c. Providing power to the devices

    d. Initiating physical actions

110. **What does load balancing refer to in IoT systems?**
    a. Distributing computational tasks evenly across devices to avoid overloading
    b. Distributing devices evenly across the network topology
    c. Distributing data storage across multiple cloud servers
    d. Distributing sensor data to devices with the highest power capacity

111. **Which IoT communication protocol is designed for real-time communication and is often used in remote control and monitoring applications?**
    a. HTTP
    b. MQTT
    c. CoAP
    d. SMTP

112. **Which IoT communication model involves direct communication between devices without involving a central server or cloud?**
    a. Device-to-cloud (D2C) communication
    b. Device-to-device (D2D) communication
    c. Device-to-gateway (D2G) communication
    d. Peer-to-peer (P2P) communication

113. **What does data normalization refer to in the context of IoT data analysis?**
    a. Processing data on the cloud server
    b. Storing data in a standardized format
    c. Converting data into a standard unit of measurement
    d. Transmitting data between devices and the cloud

114. **What does the term vulnerability assessment mean in the context of IoT security?**
    a. Initiating physical actions based on sensor data
    b. Identifying and analyzing potential weaknesses in a system
    c. Generating random data for testing purposes
    d. Processing and analyzing IoT data

115. **Which IoT communication protocol is known for its low overhead and efficient use of network resources?**
    a. HTTP
    b. MQTT
    c. SMTP
    d. CoAP

116. What is the purpose of device discovery in IoT networks?

    a. Providing energy to IoT devices

    b. Identifying devices within the network and their capabilities

    c. Processing and analyzing IoT data

    d. Initiating physical actions based on sensor data

117. What is the main function of a sensor hub in IoT devices?

    a. Initiating physical actions

    b. Collecting and processing data from multiple sensors

    c. Storing historical data

    d. Providing power to the device

118. What is the purpose of data governance in IoT systems?

    a. Initiating physical actions based on sensor data

    b. Managing device authentication

    c. Ensuring the availability of IoT devices

    d. Establishing policies and procedures for data management and usage

119. In IoT networks, what does the term endpoint refer to?

    a. The central server where data is stored and processed

    b. A device's physical location

    c. The beginning of a communication channel

    d. A device or sensor that can send or receive data

120. What is the main purpose of device configuration in IoT systems?

    a. Collecting and storing sensor data

    b. Initiating physical actions based on sensor data

    c. Setting up parameters and settings for devices

    d. Processing and analyzing IoT data

121. Which IoT architecture layer focuses on delivering data to end users and applications?

    a. Data layer

    b. Application layer

    c. Network layer

    d. Perception layer

122. **What is the primary purpose of a rule engine in IoT systems?**
    a. Initiating physical actions based on sensor data
    b. Collecting and storing sensor data
    c. Managing device authentication
    d. Processing and analyzing data based on predefined rules

123. **What is the purpose of data filtering in IoT systems?**
    a. Initiating physical actions based on sensor data
    b. Processing and analyzing data on the cloud server
    c. Storing historical data
    d. Selecting and processing relevant data from a stream of information

124. **What is the primary function of a wearable IoT device?**
    a. Initiating physical actions based on sensor data
    b. Monitoring the user's activity or health-related metrics
    c. Storing historical data
    d. Providing power to the device

125. **In the context of IoT security, what does data masking refer to?**
    a. Hiding devices from unauthorized access
    b. Encrypting data during transmission
    c. Concealing sensitive information in the database
    d. Initiating physical actions based on sensor data

126. **What is the main advantage of using mesh networking in IoT communication?**
    a. Low energy consumption
    b. High data transfer rates
    c. Centralized control
    d. Limited device scalability

127. **Which IoT architecture layer manages device communication, addressing, and routing?**
    a. Application layer
    b. Network layer
    c. Data layer
    d. Perception layer

128. **What is the primary goal of data transformation in IoT systems?**

    a. Initiating physical actions based on sensor data

    b. Collecting and storing sensor data

    c. Converting data into a standardized format

    d. Processing and analyzing IoT data

129. **In IoT security, which type of attack exploits the limited computational resources of IoT devices to force them into a state of exhaustion, leading to network failures?**

    a. Man-in-the-middle attack

    b. DoS

    c. SQL injection

    d. Cross-site scripting (XSS)

130. **What is the main purpose of over-the-air (OTA) updates in IoT systems?**

    a. Initiating physical actions based on sensor data

    b. Collecting and storing sensor data

    c. Remotely updating the firmware and software of devices

    d. Processing and analyzing IoT data

131. **In the context of IoT security, what is the purpose of tamper detection?**

    a. Encrypting data during transmission

    b. Initiating physical actions based on sensor data

    c. Identifying unauthorized access or tampering with devices

    d. Collecting and storing sensor data

132. **In IoT, the transport layer can utilize various protocols for communication. Which protocol specifically ensures reliable, ordered, and error-checked delivery of data over the network?**

    a. User Datagram Protocol (UDP)

    b. Hypertext Transfer Protocol (HTTP)

    c. Transmission Control Protocol (TCP)

    d. Message Queue Telemetry Transport (MQTT)

133. **What is the role of predictive analytics in IoT systems?**

    a. Initiating physical actions based on sensor data

    b. Collecting and storing sensor data

    c. Forecasting future events or outcomes based on historical data

    d. Processing and analyzing IoT data

134. **In IoT networks, what is the purpose of device synchronization?**

    a. Managing device authentication

    b. Collecting and storing sensor data

    c. Ensuring devices are up-to-date with the latest firmware

    d. Initiating physical actions based on sensor data

135. **What does the term embedded system refer to in the context of IoT devices?**

    a. A centralized cloud server used to store and process data

    b. A network of interconnected devices

    c. A device that can initiate physical actions based on sensor data

    d. A computing system integrated into a larger mechanical or electronic system

136. **What is the main purpose of device telemetry in IoT systems?**

    a. Initiating physical actions based on sensor data

    b. Collecting and storing sensor data

    c. Processing and analyzing IoT data

    d. Providing power to the devices

137. **What is the main goal of data deduplication in IoT data management?**

    a. Initiating physical actions based on sensor data

    b. Storing raw and unprocessed data

    c. Identifying and removing duplicate data entries

    d. Processing and analyzing IoT data

138. **Which IoT architecture layer focuses on aggregating and processing data from multiple devices before sending it to the cloud?**

    a. Network layer

    b. Application layer

    c. Perception layer

    d. Data layer

139. **In IoT networks, what is the purpose of latency optimization?**

    a. Minimizing data transfer rates

    b. Maximizing device power consumption

    c. Reducing the time delay between data transmission and reception

    d. Providing power to the devices

140. What is the main function of a protocol converter in IoT systems?

    a. Initiating physical actions based on sensor data

    b. Translating data between different communication protocols

    c. Collecting and storing sensor data

    d. Providing power to the devices

141. In IoT networks, what is the primary role of a broker in the publish-subscribe communication model?

    a. Initiating data transmission between devices

    b. Storing historical data

    c. Managing user identities and access

    d. Facilitating communication between publisher and subscriber devices

142. What does the term payload size refer to in IoT communication protocols?

    a. The energy consumption of an IoT device

    b. The physical dimensions of an IoT device

    c. The data being transmitted between devices

    d. The processing capacity of an IoT device

143. What is the purpose of a telemetry gateway in IoT systems?

    a. Initiating physical actions based on sensor data,

    b. Collecting and storing sensor data,

    c. Translating telemetry data into readable formats

    d. Providing power to the devices

144. What is a publish-subscribe model in IoT communication?

    a. Devices communicate directly with each other

    b. Devices communicate through a central server

    c. Devices communicate using a point-to-point connection

    d. Devices publish data, and other devices subscribe to receive it

145. What is the main purpose of data integration in IoT systems?

    a. Initiating physical actions based on sensor data

    b. Storing historical data

    c. Combining data from multiple sources to provide meaningful insights

    d. Collecting and storing sensor data

146. **Which of the following IoT communication protocols provides efficient, low-power, long-range communication but suffers from higher latency, making it less suitable for real-time applications?**

    a. LoRaWAN

    b. NB-IoT

    c. Bluetooth Low Energy (BLE)

    d. Zigbee

147. **What is the primary purpose of data compression in IoT systems?**

    a. Initiating physical actions based on sensor data

    b. Reducing the size of data for efficient transmission and storage

    c. Collecting and storing sensor data

    d. Enhancing device compatibility

148. **What is the purpose of data enrichment in IoT networks?**

    a. Initiating physical actions based on sensor data

    b. Storing historical data

    c. Enhancing existing data with additional information for better analysis

    d. Collecting and storing sensor data

149. **What is the main function of a telemetry data collector in IoT systems?**

    a. Initiating physical actions based on sensor data

    b. Collecting and aggregating telemetry data from multiple sources

    c. Storing historical data

    d. Providing power to the devices

150. **What type of network is typically used to connect IoT devices within a home?**

    a. Wide area network (WAN)

    b. Local area network (LAN)

    c. Personal area network (PAN)

    d. Metropolitan area network (MAN)

151. **Which of the following is an example of an IoT application?**

    a. Word processor

    b. Smart thermostat

    c. Spreadsheet software

    d. Video game

152. Which layer of the IoT architecture is responsible for data acquisition?

a. Application layer

b. Network layer

c. Perception layer

d. Transport layer

153. What is a common characteristic of IoT devices?

a. High power consumption

b. Constant human interaction

c. Ability to collect and transmit data

d. Large physical size

154. In IoT edge computing, which of the following plays a critical role in reducing latency for time-sensitive applications by processing data closer to the source?

a. Cloud servers

b. Edge nodes

c. Network routers

d. Blockchain nodes

155. Which of the following is a key enabling technology for IoT?

a. Blockchain

b. Quantum computing

c. Augmented reality

d. Machine-to-machine (M2M) communication

156. What type of sensor is used to measure temperature in IoT applications?

a. Accelerometer

b. Gyroscope

c. Thermistor

d. Photodiode

157. What does the acronym LoRa stand for in IoT networks?

a. Long range

b. Low radiation

c. Low resistance

d. Local radio

158. **Which of the following is not a common characteristic of an IoT system?**

    a. Connectivity

    b. Decentralization

    c. Autonomous decision-making

    d. Manual data collection

159. **Which of the following is an example of a wearable IoT device?**

    a. Smart TV

    b. Fitness tracker

    c. Smart refrigerator

    d. Autonomous vehicle

160. **Which layer of the IoT architecture handles communication between devices and the cloud?**

    a. Application layer

    b. Network layer

    c. Perception layer

    d. Middleware layer

161. **What does the term smart city refer to in IoT applications?**

    a. A city with a large number of IoT devices

    b. A city with advanced IT infrastructure

    c. A city that uses IoT technologies to improve urban services

    d. A city with high internet speeds

162. **Which IoT technology is used for short-range communication between devices?**

    a. Wi-Fi

    b. Zigbee

    c. Cellular

    d. Satellite

163. **Which cloud service model is most commonly used for IoT applications?**

    a. IaaS

    b. PaaS

    c. SaaS

    d. DaaS

164. **What type of data is typically collected by IoT environmental sensors?**

    a. Financial data

    b. Weather data

    c. Personal data

    d. Health data

165. **Which technology allows IoT devices to operate without a direct power source?**

    a. Battery

    b. Solar panel

    c. Energy harvesting

    d. UPS

166. **Which IoT protocol operates primarily in the 2.4 GHz frequency band?**

    a. Zigbee

    b. LoRa

    c. NB-IoT

    d. Sigfox

167. **In which layer of the IoT architecture does data filtering and processing typically occur?**

    a. Sensing layer

    b. Network layer

    c. Middleware layer

    d. Application layer

168. **Which of the following is an example of an IoT platform?**

    a. Microsoft Azure IoT

    b. Microsoft Word

    c. Adobe Photoshop

    d. Google Docs

169. **What type of sensor is used to detect motion in IoT applications?**

    a. Temperature sensor

    b. Proximity sensor

    c. Accelerometer

    d. Humidity sensor

170. **Which IoT standard focuses on device-to-device communication?**

    a. HTTP

    b. CoAP

    c. FTP

    d. SMTP

171. **Which of the following is a challenge in IoT deployment?**

    a. Unlimited power supply

    b. Network congestion

    c. Lack of data

    d. Simple integration

172. **What type of communication technology is used in vehicle-to-everything (V2X) applications?**

    a. Wi-Fi

    b. Cellular

    c. Zigbee

    d. Bluetooth

173. **Which IoT standard is specifically designed for constrained devices?**

    a. HTTP

    b. MQTT

    c. FTP

    d. CoAP

174. **Which wireless communication technology is suitable for IoT applications requiring low data rates and long battery life?**

    a. Wi-Fi

    b. Bluetooth

    c. Zigbee

    d. LTE

175. **What is the primary benefit of using IoT in industrial automation?**

    a. Increased manual labor

    b. Higher energy consumption

    c. Improved operational efficiency

    d. Increased downtime

176. Which protocol is used for IoT device discovery and communication in a local network?

    a. FTP

    b. CoAP

    c. mDNS

    d. HTTP

177. What type of IoT device is a smart meter?

    a. Wearable device

    b. Environmental sensor

    c. Energy management device

    d. Home automation device

178. Which IoT technology is used for tracking and logistics?

    a. RFID

    b. Bluetooth

    c. Wi-Fi

    d. Zigbee

179. Which layer of the IoT architecture is responsible for data transmission?

    a. Application layer

    b. Network layer

    c. Perception layer

    d. Middleware layer

180. What does the term ubiquitous computing refer to in IoT?

    a. Computing everywhere and at all times

    b. Centralized data processing

    c. High-speed internet

    d. Real-time data analysis

181. What is the purpose of an IoT middleware platform?

    a. To store data

    b. To manage and integrate various IoT devices and applications

    c. To provide internet connectivity

    d. To control actuators

182. **Which IoT technology uses short-range wireless communication for device pairing?**

    a. Bluetooth

    b. LoRaWAN

    c. NB-IoT

    d. Zigbee

183. **Which of the following is an example of an IoT actuator?**

    a. Temperature sensor

    b. Light switch

    c. Humidity sensor

    d. Proximity sensor

184. **What is a primary use of IoT in the transportation sector?**

    a. Real-time traffic monitoring

    b. Online shopping

    c. Video conferencing

    d. Financial analysis

185. **Which of the following is a challenge in IoT device management?**

    a. Easy scalability

    b. Low power consumption

    c. Data privacy and security

    d. High processing power

186. **Which communication protocol is often used for IoT device-to-cloud communication?**

    a. CoAP

    b. HTTP

    c. FTP

    d. SMTP

187. **What type of sensor is used to detect light levels in IoT applications?**

    a. Temperature sensor

    b. Gyroscope

    c. Photodiode

    d. Accelerometer

188. **Which IoT protocol is lightweight and uses a publish-subscribe model?**

    a. HTTP

    b. CoAP

    c. FTP

    d. MQTT

189. **Which type of IoT device is used for tracking physical activity?**

    a. Smart thermostat

    b. Fitness tracker

    c. Smart refrigerator

    d. Smart TV

190. **Which layer of the IoT architecture includes the devices that directly interact with the physical environment?**

    a. Application layer

    b. Network layer

    c. Perception layer

    d. Middleware layer

191. **What is the purpose of using a mesh network in IoT?**

    a. To increase power consumption

    b. To enable long-range communication

    c. To provide redundancy and reliability

    d. To reduce the number of devices

192. **Which IoT technology is commonly used in smart lighting systems?**

    a. Zigbee

    b. LoRaWAN

    c. NB-IoT

    d. Sigfox

193. **What does the term real-time processing mean in the context of IoT?**

    a. Processing data at a later time

    b. Processing data immediately as it is received

    c. Storing data for future use

    d. Analyzing historical data

194. **What type of sensor is used to detect humidity levels in IoT applications?**

    a. Temperature sensor

    b. Accelerometer

    c. Hygrometer

    d. Proximity sensor

195. **Which IoT technology is specifically designed for massive machine-type communications (mMTC)?**

    a. Wi-Fi

    b. Bluetooth

    c. NB-IoT

    d. Zigbee

196. **What is a key benefit of using IoT in supply chain management?**

    a. Increased inventory levels

    b. Real-time tracking and monitoring

    c. Higher operational costs

    d. Reduced automation

197. **Which IoT protocol is known for its simplicity and low overhead?**

    a. HTTP

    b. CoAP

    c. FTP

    d. MQTT

198. **What is the primary function of an IoT hub?**

    a. Data storage

    b. Data encryption

    c. Centralized communication management

    d. Actuator control

199. **Which IoT technology is used for long-range, low-power communication in rural areas?**

    a. Zigbee

    b. Bluetooth

    c. LoRaWAN

    d. Wi-Fi

200. What type of data do IoT health sensors typically collect?

    a. Weather conditions

    b. Financial transactions

    c. Physiological measurements

    d. Social media interactions

201. Which IoT protocol uses a binary data format for efficient data exchange?

    a. HTTP

    b. CoAP

    c. MQTT

    d. FTP

202. What is a common application of IoT in smart cities?

    a. Online gaming

    b. Intelligent traffic management

    c. Social media marketing

    d. Video streaming

203. Which layer of the IoT architecture handles user interaction and application-specific logic?

    a. Application layer

    b. Network layer

    c. Perception layer

    d. Middleware layer

204. Which IoT technology is designed for secure, reliable communication in industrial environments?

    a. Zigbee

    b. LoRaWAN

    c. NB-IoT

    d. Industrial Ethernet

205. What is a primary challenge in managing IoT data?

    a. Limited data sources

    b. Data volume and variety

    c. Low data transfer speeds

    d. Minimal data security risks

206. **Which IoT protocol is commonly used for remote device management?**

    a. FTP

    b. CoAP

    c. SNMP

    d. HTTP

207. **Which of the following is an example of an IoT edge device?**

    a. Cloud server

    b. Smart thermostat

    c. Data center

    d. Web browser

208. **What type of sensor is used to measure pressure in IoT applications?**

    a. Temperature sensor

    b. Gyroscope

    c. Barometer

    d. Photodiode

209. **Which IoT protocol is designed for efficient communication in sensor networks?**

    a. HTTP

    b. CoAP

    c. FTP

    d. SMTP

210. **What is a key benefit of using IoT in energy management?**

    a. Increased energy consumption

    b. Real-time energy usage monitoring

    c. Reduced energy efficiency

    d. Increased manual intervention

211. **What does the term machine-to-machine (M2M) communication refer to in IoT?**

    a. Communication between humans and devices

    b. Communication between devices without human intervention

    c. Communication between cloud servers

    d. Communication between data centers

212. **What is a primary use of IoT in environmental monitoring?**

    a. Online shopping

    b. Weather forecasting

    c. Social media analysis

    d. Financial trading

213. **What is a key challenge in securing IoT networks?**

    a. High processing power

    b. Complex network architecture

    c. Limited device resources

    d. Minimal data privacy concerns

214. **Which IoT protocol uses a hierarchical structure for efficient data exchange?**

    a. HTTP

    b. CoAP

    c. MQTT

    d. FTP

215. **What type of IoT device is used for monitoring air quality?**

    a. Smart thermostat

    b. Fitness tracker

    c. Air quality sensor

    d. Smart TV

216. **Which layer of the IoT architecture is responsible for data collection and aggregation?**

    a. Application layer   b. Network layer

    c. Perception layer   d. Middleware layer

217. **Which IoT protocol is known for its reliability and real-time communication capabilities?**

    a. HTTP   b. CoAP

    c. MQTT   d. FTP

218. **What is a primary use of IoT in smart buildings?**

    a. Video streaming   b. Intelligent energy management

    c. Social media marketing   d. Online gaming

Answers

Q.No.	Answers	Q.No.	Answers	Q.No.	Answers	Q.No.	Answers	Q.No.	Answers
1	b	31	d	61	d	91	c	121	b
2	a	32	c	62	c	92	b	122	d
3	c	33	a	63	d	93	c	123	d
4	c	34	b	64	c	94	c	124	b
5	d	35	c	65	b	95	d	125	c
6	c	36	b	66	b	96	b	126	a
7	c	37	d	67	c	97	c	127	b
8	c	38	c	68	d	98	c	128	c
9	c	39	b	69	b	99	b	129	b
10	a	40	a	70	c	100	d	130	c
11	b	41	b	71	c	101	b	131	c
12	c	42	a	72	c	102	c	132	c
13	c	43	d	73	c	103	a	133	c
14	b	44	b	74	c	104	c	134	c
15	c	45	c	75	b	105	c	135	d
16	d	46	d	76	c	106	c	136	b
17	c	47	c	77	c	107	d	137	c
18	c	48	d	78	c	108	c	138	a
19	b	49	b	79	a	109	b	139	c
20	d	50	a	80	b	110	a	140	b
21	c	51	b	81	d	111	b	141	d
22	d	52	a	82	d	112	b	142	c
23	d	53	c	83	d	113	c	143	b
24	d	54	c	84	d	114	b	144	d
25	b	55	c	85	b	115	d	145	c
26	c	56	d	86	b	116	b	146	a
27	d	57	a	87	d	117	b	147	b
28	c	58	c	88	d	118	d	148	c
29	b	59	b	89	d	119	d	149	b
30	c	60	c	90	b	120	c	150	b

Q.No.	Answers	Q.No.	Answers	Q.No.	Answers	Q.No.	Answers	Q.No.	Answers
151	b	166	a	181	b	196	b	211	b
152	c	167	c	182	a	197	d	212	b
153	c	168	a	183	b	198	c	213	c
154	b	169	c	184	a	199	c	214	c
155	d	170	b	185	c	200	c	215	c
156	c	171	b	186	b	201	b	216	c
157	a	172	b	187	c	202	b	217	c
158	d	173	d	188	d	203	a	218	b
159	b	174	c	189	b	204	d		
160	b	175	c	190	c	205	b		
161	c	176	c	191	c	206	c		
162	b	177	c	192	a	207	b		
163	b	178	a	193	b	208	c		
164	b	179	b	194	c	209	b		
165	c	180	a	195	c	210	b		

Join our Discord space

Join our Discord workspace for latest updates, offers, tech happenings around the world, new releases, and sessions with the authors:

https://discord.bpbonline.com

CHAPTER 3

Domain Specific IoT

Introduction

The IoT is not simply a catchall phrase for a network of interconnected gadgets and machines; it is also a highly specialized field that caters to certain fields. Regarding IoT, domain-specific means tailored to a given industry or field. Let us explore the complexities of domain-specific IoT and its relevance and use in different fields.

Grasping IoT in its domain form

The IoT is predicated on the premise that everyday things may be endowed with the ability to collect, process, and act on data generated by other sensors and actuators embedded inside them. This connectedness and intelligence, however, may take on very different forms and have very different needs depending on the sector or business at hand. Here is where application-specific IoT comes into play.

IoT-enabled fields

IoT has also spawned a new industry entirely: **Internet of Medical Things (IoMT)** in the healthcare sector. This may range from smart pill bottles that send out reminders to patients to take their medicine to more complex systems that allow for remote patient monitoring and individualized therapy based on real-time data collected by wearable devices. Precision farming is made possible via the use of IoT and agricultural technology. Some examples of domain-specific hardware in this context include automated irrigation systems, drones for agricultural monitoring, and moisture sensors for the soil. Using these tools, farmers can give their crops the optimal quantity of water, nutrients, and care to maximize productivity and longevity.

IoT has huge implications for urban administration and infrastructure in *smart cities*. Domain-specific IoT solutions for urban centers include smart lighting systems that change depending on natural light availability, waste management systems that indicate when bins are full, and traffic management solutions that optimize flow based on real-time circumstances. The primary goal of IoT implementations in the retail sector is to simplify and improve customer service. This includes smart shelves that notify when stock is low, beacon technology that offers customers personalized deals, or even smart carts that can self-check out.

Industrial Internet of Things (IIoT) refers to a subset of the Internet that is designed specifically to improve industrial operations. Traditional factories are being transformed into smart production units thanks to IIoT applications such as predictive maintenance of equipment (for reduced downtime) and real-time quality inspections (using sensors).

Role of domain-specific Internet of Things

Domain specificity in IoT solutions can achieve better adoption rates and real-world benefits because they are tailored to a given industry's specific problems and needs.

Businesses can save money by not buying generic IoT solutions and modifying them to work; instead, they can order custom-built hardware and software.

IoT devices used in custom solutions will perform at peak efficiency since they will be fine-tuned for their duties in that area.

Compliance with regulations and safety standards is essential in many fields. Domain-specific IoT solutions can be designed to adhere to these, ensuring compliance and safety.

Predicaments and things to think about

While domain-specific IoT offers many advantages, it is essential to note that such specialization can lead to challenges in integration and standardization. Integrating solutions from different vendors might be difficult because of interoperability issues. Moreover, as with other IoT systems, security is crucial, given the sensitive nature of data in many areas.

Multiple choice questions

1. **What does the term precision agriculture refer to in the context of domain-specific IoT?**

   a. Designing IoT devices for general consumer use

   b. Using IoT to optimize farming practices and crop management

   c. Developing IoT devices for healthcare applications

   d. Implementing IoT solutions for smart home automation

2. **Which domain of IoT focuses on enhancing the safety and efficiency of transportation systems?**

   a. Healthcare IoT

   b. Industrial IoT

   c. Smart cities IoT

   d. Intelligent transportation systems (ITS)

3. **What is the primary goal of the smart grid in the context of domain-specific IoT?**

   a. Monitoring personal health and wellness

   b. Optimizing manufacturing processes

   c. Improving energy distribution and management

   d. Enhancing communication between home devices

4. **What is the purpose of wearable health devices in domain-specific IoT?**

   a. Monitoring crop conditions in agriculture

   b. Managing energy consumption in smart homes

   c. Tracking personal health and fitness metrics

   d. Enhancing security in industrial environments

5. **What does smart manufacturing aim to achieve in the context of domain-specific IoT?**

   a. Monitoring air quality in cities

   b. Improving healthcare services

   c. Enhancing production processes and efficiency in factories

   d. Optimizing household energy use

6. **What is the primary focus of IoT in the retail domain?**
    a. Monitoring air quality in stores
    b. Managing energy consumption in malls
    c. Enhancing customer shopping experience and inventory management
    d. Improving manufacturing processes

7. **Which domain of IoT involves using sensors and devices to monitor and improve environmental conditions within buildings?**
    a. Agriculture IoT
    b. Healthcare IoT
    c. Building automation IoT
    d. Automotive IoT

8. **What is the purpose of smart city initiatives in the context of domain-specific IoT?**
    a. Improving healthcare delivery
    b. Developing better transit systems
    c. Optimizing manufacturing processes
    d. Monitoring crop conditions

9. **In domain-specific IoT, what is the goal of connected vehicles technology?**
    a. Enhancing manufacturing processes
    b. Monitoring air quality in cities
    c. Improving synchronization of traffic infrastructure
    d. Enabling vehicles to communicate with each other and the infrastructure

10. **What is the primary focus of smart home applications in domain-specific IoT?**
    a. Enhancing agricultural practices
    b. Monitoring industrial machinery
    c. Improving energy efficiency and convenience in residential settings
    d. Tracking personal health and fitness

11. **Which domain of IoT involves using sensors to monitor and manage water resources, such as water quality and usage?**
    a. Agriculture IoT
    b. Healthcare IoT
    c. Environmental monitoring IoT
    d. Industrial IoT

12. **What is the purpose of smart healthcare applications in domain-specific IoT?**
    a. Monitoring air quality in medical facilities
    b. Enhancing patient care and health management
    c. Managing energy consumption in hospitals
    d. Improving manufacturing processes

13. **Which domain of IoT focuses on optimizing energy consumption and efficiency in buildings and homes?**
    a. Healthcare IoT
    b. Building automation IoT
    c. Industrial IoT
    d. Automotive IoT

14. **What is the primary goal of smart metering in domain-specific IoT?**
    a. Enhancing patient care in healthcare facilities
    b. Monitoring air quality in cities
    c. Improving energy monitoring and billing accuracy
    d. Enhancing communication between home devices

15. **In domain-specific IoT, what does industrial automation aim to achieve?**
    a. Optimizing manufacturing processes and efficiency
    b. Monitoring air quality in factories
    c. Improving healthcare services
    d. Managing energy consumption in industries

16. **Which domain of IoT involves using sensors and devices to improve safety and security in public spaces?**
    a. Agriculture IoT
    b. Industrial IoT
    c. Smart cities IoT
    d. Automotive IoT

17. **What is the purpose of smart energy management in the context of domain-specific IoT?**
    a. Enhancing healthcare services
    b. Monitoring crop conditions
    c. Optimizing energy consumption and distribution
    d. Improving communication between vehicles

18. **In domain-specific IoT, what is the primary focus of connected healthcare applications?**
    a. Monitoring air quality in medical facilities
    b. Tracking personal fitness metrics
    c. Enhancing manufacturing processes
    d. Improving patient care, remote monitoring, and diagnostics

19. **What is the purpose of smart waste management in the context of domain-specific IoT?**
    a. Enhancing manufacturing processes
    b. Monitoring air quality in cities
    c. Improving healthcare services
    d. Optimizing waste collection and disposal

20. **In domain-specific IoT, what is the primary goal of smart water management solutions?**
    a. Enhancing manufacturing processes
    b. Monitoring air quality in water bodies
    c. Improving communication between vehicles
    d. Optimizing water usage, distribution, and quality monitoring

21. **Which domain of IoT involves using sensors and devices to monitor and manage air quality in urban areas?**
    a. Agriculture IoT
    b. Healthcare IoT
    c. Environmental monitoring IoT
    d. Industrial IoT

22. **In domain-specific IoT, what is the primary focus of smart building applications?**
    a. Enhancing agricultural practices
    b. Monitoring industrial machinery
    c. Improving energy efficiency and occupant comfort in commercial buildings
    d. Tracking personal health and fitness

23. **What is the purpose of smart transportation in the context of domain-specific IoT?**
    a. Enhancing healthcare services
    b. Improving communication between vehicles
    c. Optimizing traffic flow and reducing congestion
    d. Monitoring air quality in cities

24. **In domain-specific IoT, what is the goal of smart logistics technology?**

   a. Enhancing manufacturing processes

   b. Monitoring air quality in warehouses

   c. Improving communication between delivery vehicles

   d. Optimizing supply chain operations and transportation

25. **What is the primary focus of IoT in the agriculture domain?**

   a. Monitoring air quality in farms

   b. Managing energy consumption in agricultural facilities

   c. Enhancing crop management and yield optimization

   d. Improving manufacturing processes

26. **What is the primary purpose of smart lighting applications in domain-specific IoT?**

   a. Enhancing patient care in healthcare facilities

   b. Monitoring air quality in buildings

   c. Optimizing energy consumption and lighting control

   d. Improving communication between home devices

27. **Which domain of IoT involves using sensors and devices to monitor and manage air quality in homes, offices, and other buildings?**

   a. Environmental monitoring IoT

   b. Healthcare IoT

   c. Building automation IoT

   d. Industrial IoT

28. **What is the primary goal of IoT in logistics solutions?**

   a. Enhancing manufacturing processes

   b. Monitoring air quality in warehouses

   c. Improving communication between delivery vehicles

   d. Optimizing supply chain operations and transportation

29. **In domain-specific IoT, what does enhancing customer experience and operations efficiency aim to achieve?**

   a. Enhancing agricultural practices

   b. Monitoring industrial machinery

   c. Improving energy efficiency in retail spaces

   d. Tracking personal health and fitness metrics

30. **Which domain of IoT focuses on using technology to improve safety and security in industrial environments?**

    a. Smart cities IoT

    b. Environmental monitoring IoT

    c. Healthcare IoT

    d. Industrial IoT

31. **What is the purpose of smart traffic management in domain-specific IoT?**

    a. Enhancing healthcare services

    b. Improving public transportation systems

    c. Monitoring air quality in cities

    d. Optimizing traffic flow and reducing congestion

32. **In domain-specific IoT, what is the primary focus of IoT in energy applications?**

    a. Enhancing patient care in healthcare facilities

    b. Monitoring air quality in energy production facilities

    c. Managing energy consumption and distribution

    d. Improving communication between energy providers

33. **What is the primary goal of IoT in mining solutions?**

    a. Enhancing manufacturing processes

    b. Monitoring air quality in mines

    c. Improving communication between mining vehicles

    d. Optimizing mining operations and safety

34. **In domain-specific IoT, what is the purpose of smart marine technology?**

    a. Enhancing patient care in maritime facilities

    b. Monitoring air quality in ships

    c. Improving communication between vessels

    d. Enhancing safety, navigation, and operations in maritime environments

35. **Which domain of IoT involves using sensors and devices to monitor and manage air quality, noise levels, and pollution in urban areas?**

    a. Environmental monitoring IoT

    b. Healthcare IoT

    c. Smart cities IoT

    d. Industrial IoT

36. **In domain-specific IoT, what is the primary focus of IoT in aviation applications?**

    a. Enhancing manufacturing processes for aircraft

    b. Monitoring air quality in airports

    c. Improving communication between air traffic control and aircraft

    d. Optimizing flight operations, safety, and maintenance

37. **Which domain of IoT involves using sensors and devices to monitor and manage wildlife habitats and conservation areas?**

    a. Environmental monitoring IoT

    b. Healthcare IoT

    c. Industrial IoT

    d. Wildlife IoT

38. **What is the purpose of IoT in sports applications in domain-specific IoT?**

    a. Enhancing manufacturing processes for sports equipment

    b. Monitoring air quality in sports arenas

    c. Improving athlete performance and training

    d. Managing energy consumption in sports facilities

39. **In domain-specific IoT, what is the goal of smart tourism technology?**

    a. Enhancing manufacturing processes for travel-related items

    b. Monitoring air quality in tourist destinations

    c. Improving communication between travelers and service providers

    d. Optimizing tourism experiences, services, and destinations

40. **Which domain of IoT involves using sensors and devices to monitor and manage water quality and aquatic ecosystems?**

    a. Smart environmental sense

    b. Healthcare IoT

    c. Water management IoT

    d. Industrial IoT

41. **What is the primary focus of IoT in construction applications in domain-specific IoT?**

    a. Enhancing manufacturing processes for construction materials

    b. Monitoring air quality at construction sites

    c. Improving communication and efficiency in construction projects

    d. Managing energy consumption in construction equipment

42. **In domain-specific IoT, what is the purpose of smart farming technology?**
    a. Enhancing patient care in veterinary facilities
    b. Monitoring air quality in animal farms
    c. Improving communication between farmers and livestock
    d. Optimizing agricultural processes, crop management, and animal husbandry

43. **Which domain of IoT involves using sensors and devices to monitor and manage forest ecosystems, fire prevention, and wildlife protection?**
    a. Environmental monitoring IoT
    b. Wildlife conservation IoT
    c. Smart forest monitoring
    d. Industrial IoT

44. **What is the purpose of IoT in hospitality applications in domain-specific IoT?**
    a. Enhancing manufacturing processes for hospitality-related items
    b. Monitoring air quality in hotels and resorts
    c. Improving communication between guests and service providers
    d. Optimizing guest experiences, services, and facility management

45. **In domain-specific IoT, what is the goal of smart waste recycling technology?**
    a. Enhancing manufacturing processes for recycling equipment
    b. Monitoring air quality at recycling facilities
    c. Improving communication between waste collection points
    d. Optimizing recycling processes, waste separation, and resource recovery

46. **What is the primary purpose of IoT in fisheries applications in domain-specific IoT?**
    a. Enhancing manufacturing processes for fishing gear
    b. Monitoring water quality in fishing areas
    c. Improving communication between fishermen and seafood markets
    d. Optimizing fisheries management, aquatic resource monitoring, and sustainability

47. **In domain-specific IoT, what is the focus of IoT in disaster management solutions?**
    a. Enhancing manufacturing processes for emergency response equipment
    b. Monitoring air quality during disasters
    c. Improving communication and coordination among response teams
    d. Optimizing disaster preparedness, response, and recovery efforts

48. **Which domain of IoT involves using sensors and devices to monitor and manage air and water quality in aquatic environments?**

    a. Environmental monitoring IoT

    b. Healthcare IoT

    c. Aquatic ecosystem IoT

    d. Industrial IoT

49. **In domain-specific IoT, what is the purpose of IoT in cultural heritage applications?**

    a. Enhancing manufacturing processes for cultural artifacts

    b. Monitoring air quality in museums and heritage sites

    c. Improving communication between cultural institutions and visitors

    d. Optimizing preservation efforts, artifact monitoring, and visitor experiences

50. **What is the primary goal of IoT in waste-to-energy technology in domain-specific IoT?**

    a. Enhancing manufacturing processes for waste-to-energy facilities

    b. Monitoring air quality at waste-to-energy plants

    c. Improving communication between waste collection and energy generation

    d. Optimizing waste conversion processes, energy production, and environmental impact

51. **In domain-specific IoT, what is the focus of IoT in smart fishing applications?**

    a. Enhancing manufacturing processes for fishing vessels

    b. Monitoring air quality in fishing markets

    c. Improving communication between fishermen and seafood markets

    d. Optimizing fishing operations, catch monitoring, and sustainable fishing practices

52. **What is the purpose of IoT in education applications in domain-specific IoT?**

    a. Enhancing manufacturing processes for educational materials

    b. Monitoring air quality in educational institutions

    c. Enhancing teacher-student interaction

    d. Optimizing educational experiences, classroom management, and learning resources

53. **In domain-specific IoT, what is the goal of IoT in water management solutions?**

    a. Enhancing manufacturing processes for water treatment equipment

    b. Monitoring air quality in water treatment plants

    c. Improving communication between water sources and consumers

    d. Optimizing water distribution, quality monitoring, and conservation efforts

54. **Which domain of IoT involves using sensors and devices to monitor and manage air quality and noise pollution in urban and suburban areas?**

    a. Environmental monitoring IoT

    b. Healthcare IoT

    c. Smart city quality monitoring

    d. Industrial IoT

55. **What is the primary focus of IoT in disaster recovery applications in domain-specific IoT?**

    a. Enhancing manufacturing processes for recovery equipment

    b. Monitoring air quality during recovery operations

    c. Improving communication and coordination among response and recovery teams

    d. Optimizing disaster assessment, restoration, and rebuilding efforts

56. **In domain-specific IoT, what is the purpose of IoT in elderly care technology?**

    a. Enhancing manufacturing processes for elderly care equipment

    b. Monitoring air quality in nursing homes and care facilities

    c. Improving communication between caregivers and elderly individuals

    d. Optimizing elderly care services, health monitoring, and quality of life

57. **What is the primary goal of IoT in wildlife tracking applications in domain-specific IoT?**

    a. Enhancing manufacturing processes for tracking devices

    b. Monitoring air quality in wildlife habitats

    c. Improving communication between wildlife researchers and conservationists,

    d. Optimizing wildlife monitoring, species preservation, and habitat management

58. **Which domain of IoT involves using sensors and devices to monitor and manage air quality and temperature in climate-sensitive environments?**

    a. Environmental monitoring IoT

    b. Healthcare IoT

    c. Climate control IoT

    d. Industrial IoT

59. **In domain-specific IoT, what is the focus of IoT in maritime safety applications?**

    a. Enhancing manufacturing processes for maritime safety equipment

    b. Monitoring air quality on ships

    c. Improving communication between vessels and maritime authorities

    d. Optimizing maritime safety measures, navigation, and emergency response

60. **What is the purpose of IoT in renewable energy applications in domain-specific IoT?**

    a. Enhancing manufacturing processes for renewable energy equipment

    b. Monitoring air quality at renewable energy plants

    c. Improving utility-customer communication

    d. Optimizing renewable energy generation, distribution, and integration

61. **In domain-specific IoT, what is the purpose of IoT in supply chain management applications?**

    a. Enhancing manufacturing processes for supply chain equipment

    b. Monitoring air quality in supply chain facilities

    c. Improving communication and coordination among suppliers and distributors

    d. Optimizing supply chain visibility, inventory tracking, and logistics

62. **Which domain of IoT involves using sensors and devices to monitor and manage air quality, temperature, and humidity in controlled environments like greenhouses?**

    a. Environmental monitoring IoT

    b. Agriculture IoT

    c. Controlled environment IoT

    d. Industrial IoT

63. **What is the primary focus of IoT in smart cities applications in domain-specific IoT?**

    a. Enhancing manufacturing processes for urban infrastructure

    b. Monitoring air quality and traffic congestion in cities

    c. Improving communication and services in urban areas

    d. Optimizing urban planning, resource management, and citizen engagement

64. **In domain-specific IoT, what is the goal of IoT in oil and gas solutions?**

    a. Enhancing manufacturing processes for oil and gas equipment

    b. Monitoring air quality at oil and gas facilities

    c. Improving communication and safety in oil and gas operations

    d. Optimizing exploration, extraction, and distribution of oil and gas resources

65. What is the purpose of IoT in mental health applications in domain-specific IoT?

a. Enhancing manufacturing processes for mental health devices

b. Monitoring air quality in mental health facilities

c. Improving communication between mental health professionals and patients

d. Optimizing mental health assessment, support, and intervention

66. In domain-specific IoT, what is the purpose of IoT in remote monitoring solutions?

a. Enhancing manufacturing processes for remote monitoring devices

b. Monitoring air quality in remote locations

c. Improving communication and data collection from distant assets

d. Enhancing remote equipment management and diagnostics

67. What is the primary goal of IoT in sports analytics technology in domain-specific IoT?

a. Enhancing manufacturing processes for sports equipment

b. Monitoring air quality in sports arenas

c. Improving communication between athletes and coaches

d. Optimizing performance analysis, training, and strategy in sports

68. Which domain of IoT involves using sensors and devices to monitor and manage air quality and environmental factors in laboratories?

a. Environmental monitoring IoT

b. Healthcare IoT

c. Laboratory environment IoT

d. Industrial IoT

69. In domain-specific IoT, what is the focus of IoT in wildlife research applications?

a. Optimizing the manufacturing of tools used in wildlife research

b. Monitoring air quality in research stations

c. Improving communication among wildlife researchers and conservationists

d. Optimizing wildlife behavior observation, data collection, and preservation efforts

70. What is the purpose of IoT in smart water purification applications in domain-specific IoT?

a. Enhancing manufacturing processes for water purification equipment

b. Monitoring air quality in water treatment plants

    c. Improving communication and efficiency in water purification processes

    d. Optimizing water treatment, quality monitoring, and contamination detection

71. **In domain-specific IoT, what is the goal of IoT in fire prevention solutions?**

    a. Enhancing manufacturing processes for firefighting equipment

    b. Monitoring air quality and temperature in fire-prone areas

    c. Improving communication and early detection of fire hazards

    d. Optimizing fire prevention strategies, response, and emergency services

72. **Which domain of IoT involves using sensors and devices to monitor and manage air quality and environmental conditions in data centers?**

    a. Environmental monitoring IoT

    b. IT infrastructure IoT

    c. IoT-based data center monitoring

    d. Industrial IoT

73. **What is the primary focus of IoT in pest control applications in domain-specific IoT?**

    a. Enhancing manufacturing processes for pest control equipment

    b. Monitoring air quality in agricultural fields

    c. Improving communication and pest detection in farms and urban areas

    d. Optimizing pest management, prevention, and eradication efforts

74. **In domain-specific IoT, what is the purpose of IoT in disaster resilience technology?**

    a. Enhancing manufacturing processes for disaster resilience equipment

    b. Monitoring air quality during disasters

    c. Improving communication and preparedness among communities

    d. Optimizing disaster response, recovery, and community resilience

75. **What is the primary goal of IoT in home security applications in domain-specific IoT?**

    a. Enhancing manufacturing processes for security devices

    b. Monitoring air quality in homes

    c. Improving communication and surveillance in residential settings

    d. Optimizing home security systems, intrusion detection, and automation

76. **Which domain of IoT involves using sensors and devices to monitor and manage air quality, temperature, and lighting in art preservation settings?**

    a. Environmental monitoring IoT

    b. Healthcare IoT

    c. Art conservation IoT

    d. Industrial IoT

77. **In domain-specific IoT, what is the focus of IoT in marine research applications?**

    a. Enhancing manufacturing processes for marine research equipment

    b. Monitoring air quality in marine research stations

    c. Improving communication among marine researchers and conservationists

    d. Optimizing marine ecosystem monitoring, data collection, and preservation efforts

78. **What is the purpose of IoT in smart waste disposal applications in domain-specific IoT?**

    a. Enhancing manufacturing processes for waste disposal equipment

    b. Monitoring air quality in waste disposal facilities

    c. Improving communication and efficiency in waste collection and disposal

    d. Improving solid waste handling and recycling processes

79. **What is the goal of IoT in smart transportation solutions in domain-specific IoT?**

    a. Enhancing manufacturing processes for transportation vehicles

    b. Monitoring air quality in transportation hubs

    c. Improving communication and efficiency in transportation systems

    d. Improving fleet management and vehicle monitoring

80. **Which IoT domain tracks air quality, temperature, and humidity in storage units?**

    a. Environmental monitoring IoT

    b. Storage environment IoT

    c. Logistics IoT

    d. Industrial IoT

81. **What is the primary focus of IoT in disaster assessment applications in domain-specific IoT?**

    a. Enhancing manufacturing processes for disaster assessment equipment,

    b. Monitoring air quality and temperature during disasters

    c. Improving communication and data collection for rapid disaster assessment

    d. Optimizing disaster impact analysis, damage assessment, and response planning

82. **In domain-specific IoT, what is the purpose of IoT in waste management technology?**

    a. Enhancing manufacturing processes for waste management equipment

    b. Monitoring air quality in waste disposal facilities

    c. Improving communication and efficiency in waste collection and disposal

    d. Optimizing waste collection, sorting, recycling, and disposal processes

83. **What is the goal of IoT in accessibility applications in domain-specific IoT?**

    a. Enhancing manufacturing processes for accessibility devices

    b. Monitoring air quality in public spaces

    c. Improving communication and support for individuals with disabilities

    d. Optimizing accessibility in environments, products, and services

84. **In domain-specific IoT, what is the focus of IoT in air travel applications?**

    a. Enhancing manufacturing processes for aviation equipment

    b. Monitoring air quality and passenger comfort on flights

    c. Improving communication between airlines and passengers

    d. Optimizing aviation safety, passenger experiences, and operations

85. **In a smart retail IoT environment, which technology is most effective for tracking customer movement and providing personalized shopping experiences?**

    a. Bluetooth beacons

    b. NFC

    c. Wi-Fi triangulation

    d. RFID tags

86. **What is the primary purpose of IoT in waste recycling applications in domain-specific IoT?**

    a. Enhancing manufacturing processes for recycling equipment

    b. Monitoring air quality in recycling facilities

    c. Improving communication and efficiency in recycling processes

    d. Optimizing recycling practices, waste separation, and material recovery

87. **Which security concern is particularly prevalent in IoT-based healthcare systems due to the sensitivity of personal health data?**

    a. DoS relevant but less patient-data specific

    b. Data integrity attacks

    c. Man-in-the-middle (MITM) attacks

    d. Sensor spoofing

88. **In a domain-specific IoT architecture for smart manufacturing, which industrial communication protocol is most commonly used for real-time data exchange between controllers and sensors?**

    a. Modbus TCP/IP

    b. BACnet

    c. HTTP/2

    d. Factory-floor real-time controller bus

89. **In domain-specific IoT, what is the focus of IoT in asset tracking solutions?**

    a. Enhancing manufacturing processes for tracking devices

    b. Monitoring air quality in storage facilities

    c. Improving communication and visibility of assets and inventory

    d. Optimizing asset management, tracking, and utilization

90. **Which IoT domain monitors air and noise levels in public areas?**

    a. Environmental monitoring IoT

    b. Healthcare IoT

    c. Urban recreation IoT

    d. Industrial IoT

91. **What is the purpose of IoT in disaster response applications in domain-specific IoT?**

    a. Enhancing manufacturing processes for disaster response equipment

    b. Monitoring air quality and temperature during disaster recovery

    c. Improving communication and coordination of response efforts

    d. Optimizing disaster preparedness, response, and coordination

92. **In domain-specific IoT, what is the goal of IoT in waste-to-energy solutions?**

    a. Enhancing manufacturing processes for waste-to-energy equipment

    b. Monitoring air quality at waste-to-energy plants

    c. Improving communication and energy generation from waste

    d. Optimizing waste conversion processes, energy production, and sustainability

93. **What is the primary focus of IoT in maritime surveillance applications in domain-specific IoT?**

    a. Enhancing manufacturing processes for maritime surveillance equipment

    b. Monitoring air quality and sea conditions in maritime zones

    c. Improving communication and monitoring of maritime activities

    d. Optimizing maritime security, safety, and environmental monitoring

94. **Which domain of IoT involves using sensors and devices to monitor and manage air quality, temperature, and humidity in cleanroom environments like semiconductor manufacturing facilities?**

    a. Environmental monitoring IoT

    b. Smart manufacturing in semiconductor industry

    c. Cleanroom environment IoT

    d. Industrial IoT

95. **In domain-specific IoT, what is the purpose of IoT in public safety technology?**

    a. Enhancing manufacturing processes for public safety equipment

    b. Monitoring air quality in public spaces

    c. Improving communication and coordination of public safety services

    d. Optimizing public safety measures, emergency response, and crisis management

96. **What is the primary goal of IoT in tourism applications in domain-specific IoT?**

    a. Enhancing manufacturing processes for tourism-related items

    b. Monitoring air quality and crowd density in tourist destinations

    c. Improving communication and travel experiences for tourists

    d. Optimizing tourism services, attractions, and traveler satisfaction

97. **What is the focus of IoT in waste collection solutions in domain-specific IoT?**

    a. Enhancing manufacturing processes for waste collection equipment

    b. Monitoring air quality during waste collection operations

    c. Improving communication and efficiency of waste collection services

    d. Optimizing waste collection routes, schedules, and bin monitoring

98. **Which domain of IoT involves using sensors and devices to monitor and manage air quality and environmental conditions in indoor farming and hydroponic setups?**

    a. Environmental monitoring IoT

    b. Smart farming using IoT

    c. Indoor farming IoT

    d. Industrial IoT

99. **What is the purpose of IoT in disaster simulation applications in domain-specific IoT?**

    a. Enhancing manufacturing processes for disaster simulation equipment

    b. Monitoring air quality and temperature during disaster scenarios

    c. Improving communication and coordination of disaster response simulations

    d. Optimizing disaster preparedness, training, and response strategy development

100. **What is the goal of IoT in retail analytics technology in domain-specific IoT?**

    a. Enhancing manufacturing processes for retail products

    b. Monitoring air quality in retail stores

    c. Improving communication and customer behavior analysis in retail environments

    d. Improving store management and shopping experiences

101. **Which of the following is a key benefit of IoT in healthcare?**

    a. Increased patient data privacy

    b. Decreased need for medical professionals

    c. Improved patient monitoring and care

    d. Reduced cost of hospital construction

102. **What type of IoT device is commonly used for continuous glucose monitoring?**

    a. Smartwatch

    b. Smart thermostat

    c. Continuous glucose monitor (CGM)

    d. Smart speaker

103. **How does IoT enhance remote patient monitoring?**

    a. By replacing doctors with AI

    b. By automating medical surgeries

    c. By collecting real-time health data and transmitting it to healthcare providers

    d. By reducing the need for medical imaging

104. What is the primary goal of industrial IoT?

    a. To replace human workers with robots

    b. To connect industrial equipment for enhanced data collection and analysis

    c. To reduce the cost of industrial equipment

    d. To increase the number of industrial accidents

105. Which protocol is commonly used in Industrial Internet of Things (IIoT) for machine-to-machine communication?

    a. HTTP

    b. FTP

    c. Modbus TCP

    d. SMTP

106. What does predictive maintenance in IoT aim to achieve?

    a. Increase unplanned downtime

    b. Predict equipment failures before they occur

    c. Eliminate the need for regular maintenance checks

    d. Increase the cost of maintenance

107. Which of the following is an example of a smart city application?

    a. Self-driving vehicles

    b. Smart street lighting

    c. High-speed rail

    d. Traditional telephone networks

108. How can IoT improve waste management in smart cities?

    a. By using drones to collect waste

    b. By deploying smart bins that notify waste management services when they are full

    c. By reducing the number of waste collection vehicles

    d. By incinerating waste in real-time

109. What role do sensors play in smart city infrastructure?

    a. They replace human workers

    b. They collect and transmit data for better city management

    c. They increase the cost of city operations

    d. They are used solely for traffic monitoring

110. **Which IoT device is used to monitor soil moisture levels in agriculture?**

    a. Smart sprinkler

    b. Soil moisture sensor

    c. Weather station

    d. GPS tracker

111. **How does IoT help in precision farming?**

    a. By reducing the number of farm workers

    b. By providing real-time data on crop conditions

    c. By eliminating the need for pesticides

    d. By using drones for manual labor

112. **What is the main benefit of using IoT in agriculture?**

    a. Increased use of chemicals

    b. Better crop yield and resource management

    c. Reduced need for irrigation

    d. Increased manual labor

113. **How can IoT improve the customer experience in retail?**

    a. By increasing product prices

    b. By providing personalized shopping experiences

    c. By reducing the number of products available

    d. By eliminating the need for store employees

114. **Which IoT technology is often used for inventory management in retail?**

    a. Smart cameras

    b. RFID tags

    c. Smart thermostats

    d. Smart speakers

115. **What is a common application of IoT in retail stores?**

    a. Autonomous checkout systems

    b. Smart lighting systems

    c. Advanced heating systems

    d. Improved parking management

116. **Which IoT device is used for home automation?**

    a. Smart refrigerator

    b. Intelligent climate control device

    c. Smart TV

    d. Smart lighting system

117. **What is a major advantage of IoT in smart homes?**

    a. Increased electricity bills

    b. Enhanced security and convenience

    c. Reduced internet speed

    d. More complicated home management

118. **How do smart thermostats benefit homeowners?**

    a. By automatically adjusting temperature based on preferences and reducing energy consumption

    b. By making it harder to control home temperature

    c. By increasing heating costs

    d. By eliminating the need for air conditioning

119. **What is a key application of IoT in transportation?**

    a. Real-time vehicle tracking

    b. Increasing fuel consumption

    c. Reducing vehicle lifespan

    d. Minimizing traffic jams

120. **How does IoT improve fleet management?**

    a. By providing real-time data on vehicle location and performance

    b. By increasing the number of vehicles needed

    c. By eliminating the need for drivers

    d. By reducing vehicle maintenance requirements

121. **What is the primary benefit of IoT in energy management?**

    a. Increased energy consumption

    b. Enhanced energy efficiency and reduced costs

    c. Reduced need for energy sources

    d. More frequent power outages

122. Which IoT device is commonly used in smart grids?

a. Smart meter

b. Smart speaker

c. Smart camera

d. Smart refrigerator

123. How can IoT help in managing energy consumption in buildings?

a. By providing real-time data on energy usage and enabling automated control of systems

b. By increasing the need for manual monitoring

c. By reducing the availability of renewable energy sources

d. By increasing the cost of energy

124. What is a common application of IoT in environmental monitoring?

a. Smart lighting

b. Air quality monitoring

c. Smart speakers

d. Autonomous vehicles

125. How does IoT enhance environmental conservation efforts?

a. By increasing pollution levels

b. By providing real-time data on environmental conditions for better decision-making

c. By reducing the need for environmental policies

d. By increasing deforestation

126. Which IoT sensor is used to detect water pollution?

a. Temperature sensor

b. pH sensor

c. Light sensor

d. Motion sensor

127. Which of the following is a key feature of connected cars?

a. Increased fuel consumption

b. Real-time vehicle diagnostics and predictive maintenance

c. Reduced safety features

d. Manual navigation systems

128. **How does IoT improve vehicle safety?**

    a. By eliminating seat belts

    b. By providing real-time traffic data and automated emergency response

    c. By increasing the number of accidents

    d. By reducing vehicle lifespan

129. **What technology is often used in automotive IoT for vehicle-to-vehicle communication?**

    a. Wi-Fi

    b. Bluetooth

    c. C-V2X

    d. Zigbee

130. **Which IoT device is commonly used for fitness tracking?**

    a. Smart watch

    b. Smart thermostat

    c. Smart refrigerator

    d. Smart lighting system

131. **How do wearable IoT devices benefit users?**

    a. By increasing sedentary behaviour

    b. By tracking physical activity and health metrics

    c. By reducing the need for exercise

    d. By providing entertainment content

132. **Which sensor is typically found in a fitness tracker?**

    a. Temperature sensor

    b. Accelerometer

    c. Pressure sensor

    d. Light sensor

133. **How can IoT improve supply chain management?**

    a. By increasing inventory losses

    b. By providing real-time tracking of goods and inventory

    c. By reducing the need for inventory management

    d. By increasing transportation costs

134. What type of IoT technology is commonly used for tracking shipments?

    a. Smart speakers

    b. GPS trackers

    c. Smart thermostats

    d. Smart lighting systems

135. How does IoT enhance the efficiency of warehouse operations?

    a. By reducing the number of workers

    b. By providing real-time data on inventory levels and optimizing workflows

    c. By increasing manual labor

    d. By decreasing the accuracy of inventory data

136. Which IoT device helps in monitoring livestock health?

    a. Soil moisture sensor

    b. GPS tracker

    c. Smart collar

    d. Smart sprinkler

137. How does IoT contribute to sustainable agriculture practices?

    a. By increasing the use of chemical fertilizers

    b. By providing data for precise application of resources and reducing waste

    c. By decreasing crop yields

    d. By reducing the use of organic farming methods

138. Which IoT technology is used for automated irrigation in agriculture?

    a. Smart speaker

    b. Smart sprinkler system

    c. Smart thermostat

    d. Smart refrigerator

139. What is the main advantage of a smart grid?

    a. Increased power outages

    b. Enhanced energy efficiency and reliability

    c. Reduced integration of renewable energy sources

    d. Increased energy consumption

140. **Which IoT device is crucial for consumer energy monitoring in a smart grid?**

    a. Smart meter

    b. Smart TV

    c. Smart speaker

    d. Smart camera

141. **How does IoT support renewable energy integration in smart grids?**

    a. By decreasing the use of solar panels

    b. By providing real-time data on energy production and consumption

    c. By increasing the reliance on fossil fuels

    d. By reducing the efficiency of wind turbines

142. **Which IoT technology is used for automated checkout systems in retail?**

    a. Computer vision

    b. Smart thermostat

    c. Smart speaker

    d. Smart refrigerator

143. **How can IoT enhance customer engagement in retail stores?**

    a. By reducing product variety

    b. By providing personalized promotions and recommendations

    c. By increasing checkout times

    d. By eliminating customer service

144. **What role do beacons play in retail IoT?**

    a. They act as security cameras

    b. They provide location-based information and promotions to customers

    c. They manage inventory

    d. They control store lighting

145. **Which IoT device helps in home security by monitoring entrances?**

    a. Smart refrigerator

    b. Smart doorbell

    c. Smart thermostat

    d. Smart TV

146. How does a smart thermostat contribute to energy savings?

    a. By increasing heating costs

    b. By automatically adjusting the temperature based on occupancy and preferences

    c. By reducing the need for air conditioning

    d. By making manual temperature control harder

147. What is the purpose of a smart plug in a smart home?

    a. To control lighting

    b. To automate appliances and monitor energy usage

    c. To increase electricity bills

    d. To provide internet access

148. What is a primary benefit of IoT in smart manufacturing?

    a. Increased production costs

    b. Enhanced operational efficiency and reduced downtime

    c. Reduced product quality

    d. Increased manual labor

149. Which IoT device is used for real-time monitoring of manufacturing equipment?

    a. Smart TV

    b. Smart sensor

    c. Smart speaker

    d. Smart refrigerator

150. How does predictive maintenance benefit manufacturing operations?

    a. By increasing equipment failures

    b. By predicting and addressing issues before they cause downtime

    c. By reducing the lifespan of equipment

    d. By increasing the need for manual inspections

151. Which IoT device is used for remote patient monitoring?

    a. Smart TV

    b. Wearable health monitor

    c. Smart speaker

    d. Smart thermostat

152. **How does IoT improve medication adherence for patients?**

   a. By increasing the complexity of medication schedules

   b. By providing reminders and tracking medication intake

   c. By reducing the availability of medications

   d. By increasing the cost of medications

153. **What is the benefit of IoT-enabled medical devices in hospitals?**

   a. Increased risk of infections

   b. Improved patient outcomes through continuous monitoring and data collection

   c. Reduced access to patient data

   d. Increased manual data entry

154. **Which IoT sensor is used for detecting changes in temperature?**

   a. Pressure sensor

   b. Temperature sensor

   c. pH sensor

   d. Motion sensor

155. **How can IoT aid in disaster management?**

   a. By reducing the availability of emergency services

   b. By providing real-time data on environmental conditions and early warning systems

   c. By increasing the response time to disasters

   d. By decreasing the accuracy of weather predictions

156. **What is the purpose of IoT-enabled air quality monitors?**

   a. To increase air pollution

   b. To provide real-time data on air quality and pollutants

   c. To reduce the use of air purifiers

   d. To monitor water quality

157. **Which IoT technology is used for real-time traffic management?**

   a. Smart cameras

   b. Smart thermostats

   c. Smart speakers

   d. Smart refrigerators

158. How does IoT improve public transportation systems?

    a. By reducing the number of routes available

    b. By providing real-time updates on schedules and vehicle locations

    c. By increasing the cost of tickets

    d. By decreasing the reliability of services

159. What is a key benefit of IoT in vehicle telematics?

    a. Increased fuel consumption

    b. Enhanced vehicle tracking and diagnostics

    c. Reduced safety features

    d. Increased emissions

160. Which IoT device is used to monitor equipment vibration in industrial settings?

    a. Smart camera

    b. Vibration sensor

    c. Smart speaker

    d. Smart thermostat

161. How does IoT improve operational efficiency in manufacturing?

    a. By reducing the number of automated systems

    b. By providing real-time data and analytics for process optimization

    c. By increasing manual labor requirements

    d. By decreasing the use of robotics

162. What is the role of digital twins in industrial IoT?

    a. To provide entertainment content

    b. To create a virtual replica of physical assets for monitoring and simulation

    c. To replace human workers

    d. To increase production costs

163. Which IoT device can control home lighting remotely?

    a. Smart refrigerator

    b. Smart lighting system

    c. Smart thermostat

    d. Smart TV

164. **How do smart security cameras enhance home security?**

    a. By increasing the risk of break-ins

    b. By providing real-time video surveillance and alerts

    c. By reducing the availability of security systems

    d. By increasing the complexity of home networks

165. **What is the benefit of a smart home hub?**

    a. Increased electricity usage

    b. Centralized control of connected devices

    c. Reduced functionality of smart devices

    d. Increased setup complexity

166. **Which IoT device is used for smart parking solutions in cities?**

    a. Smart refrigerator

    b. Smart parking sensor

    c. Smart thermostat

    d. Smart speaker

167. **How can IoT help in managing urban traffic congestion?**

    a. By reducing the number of traffic lights

    b. By providing real-time traffic data and adaptive signal control

    c. By increasing the number of vehicles on the road

    d. By decreasing the availability of public transportation

168. **What is the role of IoT in enhancing public safety in smart cities?**

    a. By increasing crime rates

    b. By providing real-time data and analytics for emergency response

    c. By reducing the number of surveillance cameras

    d. By decreasing the efficiency of law enforcement

169. **Which IoT device is used for monitoring heart rate?**

    a. Smart thermostat

    b. Smartwatch

    c. Smart refrigerator

    d. Smart TV

170. **How do wearable IoT devices help in healthcare?**

    a. By reducing the need for regular health check-ups

    b. By providing real-time health data and alerts to users and healthcare providers

    c. By increasing the cost of healthcare

    d. By decreasing the availability of medical devices

171. **What is the benefit of IoT-enabled fitness trackers?**

    a. Increased sedentary behavior

    b. Improved tracking of physical activity and health goals

    c. Reduced access to fitness information

    d. Increased manual data entry

172. **Which IoT device helps in managing store inventory?**

    a. Smart thermostat

    b. RFID tag

    c. Smart speaker

    d. Smart refrigerator

173. **In IoT-based environmental monitoring systems, which type of sensor is typically used for detecting air pollution levels?**

    a. Piezoelectric sensors

    b. Electrochemical sensors

    c. Capacitive proximity sensors

    d. Passive infrared sensors

174. **In a smart city IoT system, which protocol is best suited for real-time vehicular-to-infrastructure (V2I) communication for optimizing traffic flow and reducing congestion?**

    a. Bluetooth 5.0

    b. LTE-M

    c. C-V2X

    d. NB-IoT

175. **Which IoT device is used for real-time tracking of goods in transit?**

    a. Smart thermostat

    b. GPS tracker

    c. Smart speaker

    d. Smart refrigerator

176. **How does IoT improve supply chain transparency?**

   a. By increasing the number of intermediaries

   b. By providing real-time data on the location and condition of goods

   c. By reducing the accuracy of inventory data

   d. By decreasing the efficiency of logistics operations

177. **What is the benefit of using IoT in warehouse management?**

   a. Increased inventory losses

   b. Enhanced tracking of inventory and optimization of storage space

   c. Reduced automation in warehouse operations

   d. Increased manual inventory counts

178. **Which IoT device helps in monitoring weather conditions for farming?**

   a. Smart sprinkler

   b. Weather station

   c. Smart thermostat

   d. Smart refrigerator

179. **How does IoT support precision agriculture?**

   a. By reducing the use of sensors

   b. By providing data-driven insights for optimized farming practices

   c. By increasing the need for manual labor

   d. By decreasing crop yields

180. **What is the role of IoT in livestock management?**

   a. Reducing the availability of animal health data

   b. Providing real-time monitoring and health tracking of livestock

   c. Increasing the cost of livestock management

   d. Decreasing the efficiency of farming operations

181. **Which IoT device helps in balancing energy supply and demand in smart grids?**

   a. Smart TV

   b. Smart meter

   c. Smart speaker

   d. Smart refrigerator

182. How does IoT contribute to energy conservation in smart grids?

    a. By increasing energy consumption

    b. By providing real-time data for optimized energy usage and distribution

    c. By reducing the integration of renewable energy sources

    d. By decreasing the reliability of energy supply

183. What is the benefit of smart meters in energy management?

    a. Increased energy consumption

    b. Accurate real-time monitoring of energy usage and automated billing

    c. Reduced access to energy data

    d. Increased manual meter readings

184. Which IoT device is used for continuous health monitoring of patients?

    a. Smart refrigerator

    b. Wearable health monitor

    c. Smart speaker

    d. Smart thermostat

185. How does IoT enhance patient care in hospitals?

    a. By reducing the availability of patient data

    b. By providing real-time health data and improving communication with healthcare providers

    c. By increasing the cost of healthcare services

    d. By decreasing the accuracy of medical records

186. What is the role of IoT in telemedicine?

    a. Reducing access to medical consultations

    b. Enabling remote diagnosis and treatment through connected devices

    c. Increasing the complexity of medical procedures

    d. Decreasing patient satisfaction

187. Which IoT device is used for monitoring air quality in smart cities?

    a. Smart thermostat

    b. Air quality sensor

    c. Smart speaker

    d. Smart refrigerator

188. How does IoT improve waste management in cities?

    a. By reducing the number of waste collection points

    b. By providing real-time data on waste levels and optimizing collection routes

    c. By increasing waste collection costs

    d. By decreasing the efficiency of waste disposal

189. What is the benefit of smart street lighting in smart cities?

    a. Increased energy consumption

    b. Automated control and energy savings through adaptive lighting

    c. Reduced visibility on streets

    d. Increased manual control requirements

190. Which IoT device is used for monitoring sleep patterns?

    a. Smart thermostat

    b. Smartwatch

    c. Smart refrigerator

    d. Smart TV

191. How do wearable IoT devices help in personal health management?

    a. By increasing the risk of health issues

    b. By providing real-time health data and personalized insights

    c. By reducing access to health information

    d. By decreasing the accuracy of health monitoring

192. What is a common use of IoT in fitness applications?

    a. Tracking physical activity and providing health insights

    b. Increasing sedentary behavior

    c. Reducing the availability of fitness data

    d. Decreasing the effectiveness of exercise routines

193. Which IoT technology is used for monitoring the condition of perishable goods during transit?

    a. Smart thermostat

    b. Temperature sensor

    c. Smart speaker

    d. Smart refrigerator

194. How does IoT enhance the efficiency of supply chain logistics?

    a. By increasing transportation costs

    b. By providing real-time data on the location and condition of shipments

    c. By reducing the accuracy of shipment tracking

    d. By decreasing the reliability of logistics operations

195. What is the benefit of using RFID tags in supply chain management?

    a. Increased manual tracking

    b. Automated tracking and management of inventory

    c. Reduced accuracy of inventory data

    d. Increased cost of inventory management

196. Which IoT device helps in monitoring soil conditions for farming?

    a. Smart sprinkler   b. Soil moisture sensor

    c. Smart thermostat   d. Smart refrigerator

197. How does IoT support sustainable farming practices?

    a. By increasing the use of chemical pesticides

    b. By providing data for the precise application of resources and reducing waste

    c. By reducing crop yields

    d. By decreasing the efficiency of farming operations

198. What is the role of IoT in crop management?

    a. Reducing the availability of crop data

    b. Providing real-time monitoring and analytics for optimized farming practices

    c. Increasing the cost of crop production

    d. Decreasing the effectiveness of farming techniques

199. Which IoT device is used for remote monitoring of energy consumption?

    a. Smart TV   b. Smart meter

    c. Smart speaker   d. Smart refrigerator

200. How does IoT facilitate demand response in smart grids?

    a. By increasing energy demand during peak hours

    b. By providing real-time data for balancing energy supply and demand

    c. By reducing the availability of renewable energy sources

    d. By decreasing the reliability of energy distribution

Answers

Q.No.	Answers	Q.No.	Answers	Q.No.	Answers	Q.No.	Answers	Q.No.	Answers
1	b	31	d	61	d	91	c	121	b
2	d	32	c	62	c	92	d	122	a
3	c	33	d	63	d	93	d	123	a
4	c	34	d	64	d	94	c	124	b
5	c	35	c	65	c	95	c	125	b
6	c	36	d	66	d	96	d	126	b
7	c	37	a	67	d	97	c	127	b
8	b	38	c	68	c	98	c	128	b
9	d	39	d	69	d	99	d	129	c
10	c	40	c	70	d	100	c	130	a
11	c	41	c	71	c	101	c	131	b
12	b	42	d	72	d	102	c	132	b
13	b	43	c	73	d	103	c	133	b
14	c	44	d	74	c	104	b	134	b
15	a	45	d	75	d	105	c	135	b
16	c	46	d	76	c	106	b	136	c
17	c	47	c	77	d	107	b	137	b
18	d	48	c	78	d	108	b	138	b
19	d	49	d	79	d	109	b	139	b
20	d	50	d	80	b	110	b	140	a
21	c	51	d	81	d	111	b	141	b
22	c	52	c	82	d	112	b	142	a
23	b	53	d	83	c	113	b	143	b
24	d	54	c	84	d	114	b	144	b
25	c	55	d	85	c	115	a	145	b
26	c	56	d	86	d	116	d	146	b
27	c	57	d	87	d	117	b	147	b
28	d	58	c	88	c	118	a	148	b
29	c	59	d	89	c	119	a	149	b
30	d	60	d	90	c	120	a	150	b

Q.No.	Answers	Q.No.	Answers	Q.No.	Answers	Q.No.	Answers	Q.No.	Answers
151	b	161	b	171	b	181	b	191	b
152	b	162	b	172	b	182	b	192	a
153	b	163	b	173	b	183	b	193	b
154	b	164	b	174	b	184	b	194	b
155	b	165	b	175	b	185	b	195	b
156	b	166	b	176	b	186	b	196	b
157	a	167	b	177	b	187	b	197	b
158	b	168	b	178	b	188	b	198	b
159	b	169	b	179	b	189	b	199	b
160	b	170	b	180	b	190	b	200	b

Join our Discord space

Join our Discord workspace for latest updates, offers, tech happenings around the world, new releases, and sessions with the authors:

https://discord.bpbonline.com

CHAPTER 4
Sensor and Actuator

Introduction

Sensors and actuators are crucial to the IoT. They are an IoT system's eyes and hands, allowing it to sense and react to changes. Understanding sensors and actuators, the core of IoT devices, is essential for anybody interested in technological change.

Sensors in IoT

Sensors monitor, record, and react to physical properties. Sensors continually collect environmental data in IoT.

The various sensor types are:

- **Environmental sensors**: Measure temperature, humidity, and pressure.
- **Proximity sensors**: Detect objects' existence or location.
- **Image and optical sensors**: Capture visual data, such as smart security system cameras.
- **Motion sensors**: Detect nearby movement.
- **Acoustic sensors**: Receive sound waves and detect noise.
- **Gas sensors**: Measure gas concentrations.

These sensors provide data to a central system or cloud after being processed by an intermediate device or edge system.

IoT actuators

Sensors collect data, and actuators act. Using data, they may regulate a mechanism or system. Basically, a sensor detects the environment, and an actuator changes it.

The various actuator types are as follows:

- Electric actuators convert electricity into mechanical motion. Example: motors and solenoids.

- Pneumatic actuators use pressurized air to move.

- Hydraulic actuators move mechanisms using hydraulic fluid.

- Magnetic or thermal actuators employ heat or magnetic fields to move.

Symbiotic relationship

The seamless coordination between sensors and actuators makes IoT really powerful. A central system evaluates real-time sensor data and transmits actuator orders based on pre-defined algorithms or AI analysis. Consider a smart watering system with soil moisture sensors that detect dry soil. Central systems receive this data and instruct actuators to activate water valves and water plants. When sensors detect enough moisture, actuators shut valves.

Some issues and considerations are as follows:

- **Power consumption**: Remote or inaccessible sensors and actuators must be energy efficient.

- **Data overload**: Processing millions of sensors' data in real time is difficult.

- **Interoperability challenges:** With several sensors and actuators from various manufacturers, interoperability is essential.

- **Security**: Like other IoT components, sensors and actuators are subject to cyberattacks.

Multiple choice questions

1. **What is the main function of a sensor in IoT?**

    a. To process data

    b. To store data

    c. To generate data

    d. To transmit data

2. **Which of the following is an example of an analog sensor?**

    a. Temperature sensor

    b. Light sensor

  c. Proximity sensor

  d. Ultrasonic sensor

3. **Which type of sensor measures distance by sending out sound waves and calculating the time it takes for them to bounce back?**

  a. Temperature sensor

  b. Light sensor

  c. Proximity sensor

  d. Ultrasonic sensor

4. **Which of the following is an example of a digital sensor?**

  a. Light sensor

  b. Proximity sensor

  c. Ultrasonic sensor

  d. Temperature sensor

5. **Which actuator is commonly used to control the opening and closing of valves in industrial processes?**

  a. Servo motor

  b. Solenoid

  c. Stepper motor

  d. Linear actuator

6. **Which type of actuator is known for its precise control of angular position and speed in robotics and automation?**

  a. Servo motor

  b. Solenoid

  c. Stepper motor

  d. Linear actuator

7. **Which actuator is used to convert electrical signals into mechanical movement in a linear direction?**

  a. Servo motor

  b. Solenoid

  c. Stepper motor

  d. Linear actuator

8. **Which component of an IoT system is responsible for converting physical quantities into electrical signals?**

    a. Gateway

    b. Cloud server

    c. Sensor

    d. Actuator

9. **What is the purpose of a temperature sensor in an IoT application?**

    a. To control actuators

    b. To store data

    c. To process data

    d. To measure temperature

10. **Which type of sensor is used to detect the presence or absence of an object without physical contact?**

    a. Temperature sensor

    b. Light sensor

    c. Proximity sensor

    d. Ultrasonic sensor

11. **Which actuator is commonly used to control the movement of robotic arms and CNC machines?**

    a. Servo motor

    b. Solenoid

    c. Stepper motor

    d. Linear actuator

12. **Which component of an IoT system is responsible for executing physical actions based on data inputs?**

    a. Gateway

    b. Cloud server

    c. Sensor

    d. Actuator

13. **Which type of sensor is used to measure the distance between the sensor and an object by emitting and receiving infrared light?**

    a. Temperature sensor

    b. Light sensor

c. Proximity sensor

d. Ultrasonic sensor

14. **What is the main function of a light sensor in IoT?**

    a. To control actuators

    b. To store data

    c. To process data

    d. To measure light intensity

15. **Which component of an IoT system is responsible for connecting IoT devices to the internet and enabling communication between them?**

    a. Gateway

    b. Cloud server

    c. Sensor

    d. Actuator

16. **Which type of sensor is commonly used to measure air pressure and altitude in weather monitoring applications?**

    a. Temperature sensor

    b. Light sensor

    c. Pressure sensor

    d. Ultrasonic sensor

17. **What is the main function of a pressure sensor in IoT?**

    a. To control actuators

    b. To store data

    c. To process data

    d. To measure pressure

18. **Which type of sensor is used to detect the presence of flames and heat sources in fire detection systems?**

    a. Temperature sensor

    b. Flame sensor

    c. Proximity sensor

    d. Ultrasonic sensor

19. **What is the main function of a flame sensor in IoT?**

    a. To control actuators

    b. To store data

    c. To process data

    d. To detect flames and heat sources

20. **Which type of actuator is commonly used in HVAC systems to control the flow of air or fluids?**

    a. Servo motor

    b. Solenoid

    c. Valve actuator

    d. Linear actuator

21. **What is the main function of a valve actuator in IoT?**

    a. To generate data

    b. To control valves and fluid flow

    c. To process data

    d. To measure pressure

22. **Which type of sensor is used to measure the level of liquids, powders, or granular materials in containers?**

    a. Temperature sensor

    b. Light sensor

    c. Level sensor

    d. Ultrasonic sensor

23. **What is the main function of a level sensor in IoT?**

    a. To control actuators

    b. To measure light intensity

    c. To process data

    d. To measure the level of materials in containers

24. **Which type of actuator is commonly used to control the movement of doors, gates, and hatches?**

    a. Servo motor

    b. Solenoid

    c. Linear actuator

    d. Door actuator

25. **What is the main function of a door actuator in IoT?**

    a. To control actuators

    b. To generate data

    c. To process data

    d. To perform actions based on data

26. **Which type of sensor is commonly used to detect motion and occupancy in buildings and security systems?**

    a. Temperature sensor

    b. Light sensor

    c. Motion sensor

    d. Ultrasonic sensor

27. **What is the main function of a motion sensor in IoT?**

    a. To control actuators

    b. To measure motion speed

    c. To process data

    d. To detect movement or occupancy

28. **Which component of an IoT system is responsible for processing and analyzing data collected from sensors?**

    a. Gateway

    b. Cloud server

    c. Sensor

    d. Actuator

29. **Which type of sensor is used to detect changes in magnetic fields and is commonly found in compasses and navigation systems?**

    a. Temperature sensor

    b. Light sensor

    c. Magnetic sensor

    d. Ultrasonic sensor

30. **What is the main function of a magnetic sensor in IoT?**

    a. To control actuators

    b. To measure magnetic fields

    c. To process data

    d. To detect changes in magnetic fields

31. **Which type of sensor is commonly used to measure the concentration of gases in the air, such as carbon dioxide or methane?**

    a. Temperature sensor

    b. Gas sensor

    c. Proximity sensor

    d. Ultrasonic sensor

32. **What is the main function of a gas sensor in IoT?**

    a. To control actuators

    b. To measure gas concentrations

    c. To process data

    d. To detect gas leaks

33. **Which actuator is commonly used to control the movement of camera lenses and autofocus mechanisms in photography equipment?**

    a. Servo motor

    b. Solenoid

    c. Stepper motor

    d. Lens actuator

34. **What is the main function of a stepper motor in IoT?**

    a. To control actuators

    b. To store data

    c. To generate data

    d. To provide precise angular movement

35. **Which type of sensor is used to measure the pH level of liquids, such as water, in industrial and environmental monitoring applications?**

    a. Temperature sensor

    b. pH sensor

    c. Proximity sensor

    d. Ultrasonic sensor

36. **What is the main function of a pH sensor in IoT?**

    a. To control actuators

    b. To measure pH levels

    c. To process data

    d. To measure air pressure

37. **Which actuator is commonly used to control the movement of robotic arms and grippers in manufacturing and automation processes?**

    a. Servo motor

    b. Solenoid

    c. Stepper motor

    d. Robotic actuator

38. **What is the main function of a robotic actuator in IoT?**

    a. To control actuators

    b. To generate data

    c. To process data

    d. To provide precise movement for robotic applications

39. **Which type of sensor is used to measure electrical current passing through a circuit and is commonly used for energy monitoring?**

    a. Temperature sensor

    b. Current sensor

    c. Light sensor

    d. Ultrasonic sensor

40. **What is the main function of a current sensor in IoT?**

    a. To control actuators

    b. To measure electrical current

    c. To process data

    d. To measure air quality

41. **Which component of an IoT system is responsible for transmitting data from sensors to the cloud or other devices?**

    a. Gateway

    b. Cloud server

    c. Sensor

    d. Actuator

42. **Which type of sensor is commonly used to detect and measure the concentration of pollutants and gases in the environment?**

    a. Temperature sensor

    b. Gas sensor

    c. Light sensor

    d. Ultrasonic sensor

43. **What is the main function of a gas sensor in IoT?**

    a. To control actuators

    b. To measure gas concentrations

    c. To process data

    d. To detect changes in air pressure

44. **Which actuator is commonly used to control the movement of robotic joints and limbs in humanoid robots and exoskeletons?**

    a. Servo motor

    b. Solenoid

    c. Stepper motor

    d. Robotic actuator

45. **What is the main function of a robotic actuator in IoT?**

    a. To control actuators

    b. To generate data

    c. To process data

    d. To provide precise movement for robotic applications

46. **Which type of sensor measures the presence and concentration of humidity in the air?**

    a. Temperature sensor

    b. Humidity sensor

    c. Proximity sensor

    d. Ultrasonic sensor

47. **What is the main function of a humidity sensor in IoT?**

    a. To control actuators

    b. To measure humidity levels

    c. To process data

    d. To measure magnetic fields

48. **Which actuator is commonly used to control the movement of robotic grippers and mechanical arms in industrial automation?**

    a. Servo motor

    b. Solenoid

    c. Stepper motor

    d. Robotic actuator

49. **Which of the following best describes the function of a thermocouple sensor in an IoT system?**

    a. Measures changes in the electrical resistance of a material in response to pressure

    b. Generates a voltage based on the temperature difference across two junctions

    c. Uses light waves to detect temperature variations in remote locations

    d. Converts mechanical displacement into electrical signals

50. **Which type of sensor is used to measure the speed of rotation of an object and is commonly found in automotive applications?**

    a. Temperature sensor

    b. Speed sensor

    c. Light sensor

    d. Ultrasonic sensor

51. **What is the main function of a speed sensor in IoT?**

    a. To control actuators

    b. To measure the speed of rotation

    c. To process data

    d. To measure air quality

52. **In IoT applications, capacitive touch sensors are often preferred over resistive touch sensors for which of the following reasons?**

    a. They are less responsive to environmental noise

    b. They support multi-touch functionality and higher sensitivity

    c. They are cheaper to manufacture and easier to deploy

    d. They require more force to detect user input

53. **In an IoT-enabled heating, ventilation, and air conditioning (HVAC) system, what role does an actuator play?**

    a. It detects the ambient temperature and adjusts the settings accordingly

    b. It controls the fan speed and airflow by receiving commands from a central controller

    c. It monitors humidity levels and sends data to a remote server

    d. It senses pollutants in the air and adjusts ventilation parameters

54. **Which type of sensor is used to measure the angle of rotation and is commonly found in robotic joints and control systems?**

    a. Temperature sensor

    b. Angle sensor

    c. Light sensor

    d. Ultrasonic sensor

55. **What is the main function of an angle sensor in IoT?**

    a. To control actuators

    b. To measure angles of rotation

    c. To process data

    d. To measure air pressure

56. **Which type of sensor is commonly used to measure the level of liquid in a container and is often used in tank monitoring systems?**

    a. Temperature sensor

    b. Level sensor

    c. Light sensor

    d. Ultrasonic sensor

57. **Which actuator is commonly used to control the movement of robotic fingers and grippers in prosthetic devices?**

    a. Servo motor

    b. Solenoid

    c. Stepper motor

    d. Robotic actuator

58. **Which of the following statements about micro-electro-mechanical systems (MEMS) sensors in IoT is correct?**

    a. They are large, power-hungry sensors suited for industrial applications only

    b. They are composed of miniaturized mechanical and electrical components in a single chip

    c. They can only be used in temperature and humidity sensing applications

    d. They are rarely used in wearable IoT devices due to bulkiness

59. **Which type of sensor is used to measure the acceleration of an object and is commonly found in smartphones and automotive safety systems?**

    a. Temperature sensor

    b. Acceleration sensor

    c. Light sensor

    d. Ultrasonic sensor

60. **What is the main function of an acceleration sensor in IoT?**

    a. To control actuators

    b. To measure acceleration

    c. To process data

    d. To measure magnetic fields

61. **Which actuator is commonly used to control the opening and closing of air vents in HVAC systems?**

    a. Servo motor

    b. Solenoid

    c. Stepper motor

    d. HVAC actuator

62. **What is the main function of an HVAC actuator in IoT?**

    a. To control actuators

    b. To generate data

    c. To process data

    d. To regulate airflow in HVAC systems

63. **Which type of sensor is used to measure the force applied to an object and is commonly found in industrial automation and robotics?**

    a. Temperature sensor

    b. Force sensor

    c. Light sensor

    d. Ultrasonic sensor

64. **What is the main function of a force sensor in IoT?**

    a. To control actuators

    b. To measure applied force

    c. To process data

    d. To measure air quality

65. **Which actuator is commonly used to control the movement of robotic arms and limbs in medical surgery and rehabilitation devices?**

    a. Servo motor

    b. Solenoid

    c. Stepper motor

    d. Robotic actuator

66. **Which of the following is a unique feature of piezoelectric sensors in IoT applications?**

    a. They generate a digital signal output for precise readings

    b. They require an external power source to measure vibrations

    c. They generate a voltage in response to applied pressure

    d. They can only measure humidity and temperature

67. **Which type of sensor is used to detect temperature changes and is commonly used in weather stations and climate control systems?**

    a. Temperature sensor

    b. Heat sensor

    c. Light sensor

    d. Ultrasonic sensor

68. **What is the primary advantage of using ultrasonic sensors over IR sensors for distance measurement in IoT robotics applications?**

    a. Ultrasonic sensors are unaffected by ambient light conditions

    b. Ultrasonic sensors provide higher accuracy in daylight conditions

    c. Ultrasonic sensors have a shorter range than IR sensors

    d. Ultrasonic sensors are less responsive to temperature changes

69. **Which type of sensor is used to detect the presence and activity of objects in a defined area and is commonly used in security systems?**

    a. Temperature sensor

    b. Motion sensor

    c. Light sensor

    d. Ultrasonic sensor

70. **What is the main function of a motion sensor in IoT?**

    a. To control actuators

    b. To detect motion and movement

    c. To process data

    d. To measure air quality

71. **Which actuator is commonly used to control the movement of valves and dampers in industrial processes and fluid control systems?**

    a. Servo motor

    b. Solenoid

    c. Stepper motor

    d. Valve actuator

72. **What is the main function of a valve actuator in IoT?**

    a. To control actuators

    b. To generate data

    c. To process data

    d. To control the movement of valves and dampers

73. **Which type of sensor is used to measure the position of an object along a linear path and is commonly found in industrial automation and robotics?**

    a. Temperature sensor

    b. Position sensor

    c. Light sensor

    d. Ultrasonic sensor

74. **What is the main function of a position sensor in IoT?**

    a. To control actuators

    b. To measure object position

    c. To process data

    d. To measure magnetic fields

75. **Which type of sensor is used to measure the sound intensity in the environment and is commonly found in noise monitoring applications?**

    a. Temperature sensor

    b. Sound sensor

    c. Light sensor

    d. Ultrasonic sensor

76. **What is the main function of a sound sensor in IoT?**

    a. To control actuators

    b. To measure sound intensity

    c. To process data

    d. To detect motion

77. **Which actuator is commonly used to control the movement of blinds, curtains, and shades in smart home automation systems?**

    a. Servo motor

    b. Solenoid

    c. Stepper motor

    d. Window actuator

78. **What is the main function of a window actuator in IoT?**

    a. To control actuators

    b. To generate data

    c. To process data

    d. To control the movement of blinds and curtains

79. **Which type of sensor is used to measure the distance between the sensor and an object by emitting and receiving radio waves?**

    a. Temperature sensor

    b. Radar sensor

    c. Proximity sensor

    d. Ultrasonic sensor

80. **What is the main function of a radar sensor in IoT?**

    a. To control actuators

    b. To measure distance using radio waves,

    c. To process data

    d. To detect magnetic fields

81. **Which type of sensor is used to detect the presence and concentration of volatile organic compounds (VOCs) in the air?**

    a. Temperature sensor

    b. VOC sensor

    c. Light sensor

    d. Ultrasonic sensor

82. **What is the main function of a VOC sensor in IoT?**

    a. To control actuators

    b. To measure VOC concentration

    c. To process data

    d. To detect motion

83. **Which actuator is commonly used to control the movement of robotic arms and end-effectors in manufacturing and assembly lines?**

    a. Servo motor

    b. Solenoid

    c. Stepper motor

    d. Robotic actuator

84. **Which of the following best describes the operation of a servo motor as an actuator in IoT applications?**

    a. It is designed to rotate 360° continuously in one direction

    b. It provides high torque at low speeds and can maintain a specific angle

    c. It is used primarily in audio applications for sound generation

    d. It cannot be controlled wirelessly in IoT systems

85. **Which type of sensor is used to measure the oxygen concentration in the air and is commonly found in medical devices and industrial processes?**

    a. Temperature sensor

    b. Oxygen sensor

    c. Light sensor

    d. Ultrasonic sensor

86. **What is the main function of an oxygen sensor in IoT?**

    a. To control actuators

    b. To measure oxygen concentration

    c. To process data

    d. To measure magnetic fields

87. **Which type of sensor is typically used in IoT-enabled smart buildings to detect carbon dioxide (CO_2) levels for air quality control?**

    a. Thermostat

    b. PIR sensor

    c. Chemical gas sensor

    d. Hall effect sensor

88. **Which type of sensor is used to measure the speed and direction of wind and is commonly found in weather stations and environmental monitoring?**

    a. Temperature sensor

    b. Anemometer

    c. Light sensor

    d. Ultrasonic sensor

89. **What is the main function of an anemometer in IoT?**

    a. To control actuators

    b. To measure wind speed and direction

    c. To process data

    d. To measure air pressure

90. **In a smart factory setting, which type of actuator is most suitable for automating the movement of robotic arms?**

    a. Pneumatic actuator

    b. Thermoelectric actuator

    c. Magnetic reed actuator

    d. Phototransistor actuator

91. **What distinguishes a capacitive sensor from a resistive sensor in IoT touch applications?**

    a. Capacitive sensors require direct physical contact with conductive material

    b. Resistive sensors can operate without physical contact

    c. Capacitive sensors detect changes in electric fields, making them more sensitive

    d. Resistive sensors have better accuracy in multi-touch applications

92. **Which type of sensor is used to measure an object's angle of inclination, and tilt and is commonly found in electronic devices?**

    a. Temperature sensor

    b. Tilt sensor

    c. Light sensor

    d. Ultrasonic sensor

93. **What is the main function of a tilt sensor in IoT?**

    a. To control actuators

    b. To measure the angle of inclination

    c. To process data

    d. To measure air quality

94. **Which actuator is commonly used to control the movement of robotic arms and grippers in pick-and-place applications?**

    a. Servo motor

    b. Solenoid

    c. Stepper motor

    d. Robotic actuator

95. **Which sensor is commonly used to detect gas leaks in IoT-enabled industrial safety systems?**

    a. Humidity sensor

    b. Hall effect sensor

    c. MQ gas sensor

    d. Optical sensor

96. **What is the main function of a luminosity sensor in IoT?**

    a. To control actuators

    b. To measure light intensity

    c. To process data

    d. To detect motion

97. **In IoT water quality monitoring systems, what role does a pH sensor play?**

    a. It monitors dissolved oxygen in the water

    b. It measures the acidity or alkalinity of the water

    c. It detects heavy metal contaminants in the water

    d. It controls the flow of water in the system

98. **Which of the following describes the function of a load cell in an IoT-enabled weighing system?**

    a. It measures the angle of a rotating object

    b. It senses the pressure applied to a surface

    c. It converts force into electrical signals for measuring weight

    d. It detects sound waves in the environment

99. **Which type of sensor is used to detect the presence and concentration of smoke and particulate matter in the air?**

    a. Temperature sensor

    b. Smoke sensor

    c. Light sensor

    d. Ultrasonic sensor

100. **What is the main function of a smoke sensor in IoT?**

    a. To control actuators

    b. To measure smoke concentration

    c. To process data

    d. To detect motion

101. **What is the function of a servo actuator in an IoT system controlling window blinds?**

    a. It opens and closes the blinds with precise angle control

    b. It monitors temperature and adjusts the blinds accordingly

    c. It measures light intensity to determine the position of the blinds

    d. It sends data to a central system on the position of the blinds

102. **Which type of sensor is used to measure the concentration of specific gases in the air, such as carbon monoxide or ammonia?**

    a. Temperature sensor

    b. Gas sensor

    c. Light sensor

    d. Ultrasonic sensor

103. **In a smart agricultural IoT system, which combination of sensors would be ideal for monitoring soil conditions?**

    a. Temperature sensor and PIR sensor

    b. Soil moisture sensor and pH sensor

    c. Humidity sensor and gyroscope

    d. Pressure sensor and light sensor

104. **Which type of sensor is used to detect the presence and concentration of moisture in the environment?**

    a. Temperature sensor

    b. Moisture sensor

    c. Light sensor

    d. Ultrasonic sensor

105. **What is the primary function of a moisture sensor in IoT?**

    a. To control actuators

    b. To measure moisture concentration

    c. To process data

    d. To detect motion

106. **What is the primary function of an interface electronic circuit in IoT devices?**

    a. To manage power consumption

    b. To enable communication between different modules

    c. To store data

    d. To run applications

107. **Which component is commonly used for analog-to-digital conversion in IoT devices?**

    a. Microcontroller

    b. Analog-to-digital converter (ADC)

    c. Digital-to-analog converter (DAC)

    d. Sensor

108. **What does GPIO stand for in the context of microcontrollers?**

    a. General Power Input Output

    b. General Purpose Input Output

    c. General Purpose Integrated Output

    d. General Power Integrated Output

109. **Which communication protocol is commonly used for short-range wireless communication in IoT?**

    a. UART

    b. SPI

    c. Bluetooth

    d. I2C

110. **What is the function of a pull-up resistor in an electronic circuit?**

    a. To increase current

    b. To ensure a known state for a signal line

    c. To decrease voltage

    d. To amplify a signal

111. **In an IoT application, which interface would be most suitable for connecting a temperature sensor?**

    a. USB

    b. SPI

    c. I2C

    d. HDMI

112. **Which type of sensor provides data in digital format directly?**

    a. Analog sensor

    b. Digital sensor

    c. Capacitive sensor

    d. Resistive sensor

113. **What is the primary use of a multiplexer in an IoT system?**

    a. To convert digital signals to analog

    b. To select one of many inputs

    c. To amplify signals

    d. To store data

114. **Which interface is commonly used for long-range communication in IoT applications?**

    a. Bluetooth

    b. Zigbee

    c. Wi-Fi

    d. LoRaWAN

115. **What does UART stand for in serial communication?**

    a. Universal Analog Receiver Transmitter

    b. Universal Asynchronous Receiver Transmitter

    c. Unified Asynchronous Receiver Transmitter

    d. Universal Advanced Receiver Transmitter

116. **Which component in an IoT device is responsible for executing control algorithms?**

    a. Sensor

    b. Actuator

    c. Microcontroller

    d. Power supply

117. **What is the purpose of an operational amplifier in electronic circuits?**

    a. To convert analog signals to digital

    b. To amplify voltage signals

    c. To store data

    d. To provide power

118. **Which of the following is a digital communication protocol used for sensor interfacing?**

    a. SPI

    b. PWM

    c. RTC

    d. PLL

119. **Which type of memory is often used to store firmware in IoT devices?**

    a. RAM

    b. ROM

    c. Flash memory

    d. Cache memory

120. **What does I2C stand for in communication protocols?**

    a. Inter-Integrated Circuit

    b. Intelligent Integrated Circuit

    c. Integrated Interface Communication

    d. Internal Integrated Circuit

121. **In IoT, which component is used to provide feedback from the physical environment?**

    a. Actuator

    b. Microcontroller

    c. Sensor

    d. Transistor

122. **Which type of interface is typically used for high-speed communication between microcontroller and peripherals?**

    a. UART

    b. I2C

    c. SPI

    d. GPIO

123. **What is the main advantage of using a digital sensor over an analog sensor in IoT?**

    a. Lower cost

    b. Better precision

    c. Easier integration with microcontrollers

    d. Higher power consumption

124. **Which of the following components can be used to store data temporarily in IoT devices?**

    a. Flash memory

    b. EEPROM

    c. SRAM

    d. ROM

125. **Which interface is often used for connecting external memory to a microcontroller?**

    a. USB

    b. UART

    c. SPI

    d. GPIO

126. **What does ADC stand for in the context of IoT?**

 a. Analog to digital converter

 b. Automatic data converter

 c. Analog data communicator

 d. Automatic digital communicator

127. **Which sensor type requires an operational amplifier for signal conditioning before interfacing with a microcontroller?**

 a. Digital sensor

 b. Capacitive sensor

 c. Analog sensor

 d. Proximity sensor

128. **Which interface is known for its simplicity and low pin count in IoT applications?**

 a. I2C

 b. SPI

 c. UART

 d. GPIO

129. **What is the primary advantage of using a DAC in an IoT system?**

 a. To convert digital signals to analog

 b. To increase data transmission speed

 c. To reduce power consumption

 d. To store data

130. **Which protocol is commonly used for wired communication in industrial IoT?**

 a. Wi-Fi

 b. Ethernet

 c. Bluetooth

 d. Zigbee

131. **In the context of IoT, what does PWM stand for?**

 a. Pulse Width Modulation

 b. Power Width Modulation

 c. Pulse Width Multiplication

 d. Power Width Multiplication

132. **Which type of communication protocol is LoRaWAN?**
    a. Short-range wireless
    b. Long-range wireless
    c. Wired
    d. Infrared

133. **Which component can be used to protect an IoT device from voltage spikes?**
    a. Capacitor
    b. Resistor
    c. Diode
    d. Inductor

134. **What is the function of a voltage regulator in IoT circuits?**
    a. To increase voltage
    b. To decrease voltage
    c. To maintain a constant voltage
    d. To convert AC to DC

135. **Which type of memory is non-volatile and used for long-term data storage in IoT devices?**
    a. SRAM
    b. DRAM
    c. Flash memory
    d. Cache memory

136. **Which sensor interface is known for its robustness and simplicity?**
    a. UART
    b. SPI
    c. I2C
    d. GPIO

137. **What is the main function of a capacitor in an electronic circuit?**
    a. To store energy
    b. To amplify signals
    c. To convert signals
    d. To protect against voltage spikes

138. **In an IoT system, what is the role of a microcontroller?**

    a. To sense data

    b. To perform computational tasks

    c. To provide power

    d. To store data

139. **Which communication protocol uses a master-slave architecture for communication?**

    a. I2C

    b. UART

    c. USB

    d. Ethernet

140. **Which component is used to detect physical phenomena and convert them into electrical signals in an IoT device?**

    a. Actuator

    b. Sensor

    c. Microcontroller

    d. Capacitor

141. **In an IoT circuit, what is the purpose of a crystal oscillator?**

    a. To regulate voltage

    b. To store energy

    c. To provide a clock signal

    d. To amplify signals

142. **Which interface would you use to connect a display module to a microcontroller in an IoT device?**

    a. SPI

    b. I2C

    c. UART

    d. GPIO

143. **What is the main advantage of using flash memory in IoT devices?**

    a. High speed

    b. Volatility

    c. Low power consumption

    d. Non-volatility

144. **Which component in an IoT system is responsible for data transmission over the internet?**

    a. Microcontroller

    b. Transceiver

    c. Sensor

    d. Actuator

145. **Which communication protocol is typically used for device-to-device communication in a mesh network?**

    a. Wi-Fi

    b. Zigbee

    c. Bluetooth

    d. LTE

146. **In an IoT application, what is the role of a real-time clock (RTC)?**

    a. To manage power consumption

    b. To provide accurate timekeeping

    c. To amplify signals

    d. To convert signals

147. **Which type of resistor changes its resistance with temperature?**

    a. Fixed resistor

    b. Variable resistor

    c. Thermistor

    d. Photoresistor

148. **What is the primary use of an accelerometer in an IoT device?**

    a. To measure temperature

    b. To measure acceleration

    c. To measure humidity

    d. To measure pressure

149. **Which interface is commonly used for real-time communication in IoT applications?**

    a. UART

    b. I2C

    c. SPI

    d. CAN bus

150. **What is the main purpose of using an interrupt in a microcontroller?**

    a. To increase clock speed

    b. To respond immediately to external events

    c. To store data

    d. To manage power consumption

151. **Which component is used to convert light into electrical signals in an IoT sensor?**

    a. Photodiode

    b. Thermistor

    c. Accelerometer

    d. Capacitor

152. **What is the main advantage of using SPI over I2C in IoT applications?**

    a. Lower power consumption

    b. Higher speed

    c. Simplicity

    d. Lower cost

153. **In an IoT system, what is the function of a relay?**

    a. To amplify signals

    b. To store data

    c. To switch electrical circuits

    d. To measure temperature

154. **Which communication protocol is most suitable for high-speed data transfer in IoT?**

    a. UART

    b. I2C

    c. SPI

    d. LoRaWAN

155. **What is the purpose of a watchdog timer in a microcontroller?**

    a. To regulate power

    b. To reset the system in case of failure

    c. To store data

    d. To amplify signals

156. **What is the function of a capacitor in a power supply circuit?**
    a. To store energy
    b. To regulate voltage
    c. To convert signals
    d. To amplify signals

157. **Which type of communication protocol is MQTT designed for?**
    a. Real-time communication
    b. Machine-to-machine communication
    c. Long-range communication
    d. Wired communication

158. **What is the main purpose of using a pull-down resistor in an electronic circuit?**
    a. To increase current
    b. To ensure a known state for a signal line
    c. To decrease voltage
    d. To amplify a signal

159. **Which type of interface is commonly used to connect sensors to a microcontroller in IoT applications?**
    a. HDMI
    b. USB
    c. I2C
    d. Ethernet

160. **In an IoT device, what is the role of a voltage divider?**
    a. To amplify voltage
    b. To reduce voltage
    c. To store energy
    d. To convert signals

161. **Which component is responsible for controlling the flow of current in an electronic circuit?**
    a. Capacitor
    b. Resistor
    c. Transistor
    d. Inductor

162. **In IoT, which wireless technology operates in the 2.4 GHz frequency band?**

    a. Wi-Fi

    b. Bluetooth

    c. Zigbee

    d. All of the above

163. **What is the main purpose of using a diode in an electronic circuit?**

    a. To amplify signals

    b. To convert AC to DC

    c. To store energy

    d. To regulate voltage

164. **What is the main advantage of using a microcontroller in IoT devices?**

    a. High power consumption

    b. High cost

    c. Flexibility and programmability

    d. Large size

165. **Which of the following is a key characteristic of smart sensors?**

    a. High power consumption

    b. Data processing capabilities

    c. Limited connectivity

    d. No data storage

166. **In IoT, what role do smart sensors primarily play?**

    a. Actuators

    b. Data acquisition

    c. Data storage

    d. Data visualization

167. **What technology enables smart sensors to communicate wirelessly?**

    a. Zigbee

    b. HDMI

    c. USB

    d. Ethernet

168. In IoT, what is a common use of humidity sensors?

    a. Measuring speed

    b. Monitoring indoor air quality

    c. Detecting sound

    d. Tracking location

169. Which sensor type is used for proximity detection?

    a. Gyroscope

    b. Infrared sensor

    c. Barometer

    d. Hygrometer

170. What does an RFID sensor use to identify objects?

    a. Optical signals

    b. Sound waves

    c. Radio waves

    d. Magnetic fields

171. Which sensor is commonly used in smartwatches to monitor heart rate?

    a. Pressure sensor

    b. Photoplethysmogram (PPG) sensor

    c. Magnetometer

    d. Thermistor

172. Which of the following is not a feature of a smart sensor?

    a. Data logging

    b. Autonomous decision making

    c. Cloud connectivity

    d. Physical switches

173. Which type of sensor is used to measure the distance to an object?

    a. Temperature sensor

    b. Proximity sensor

    c. Lidar sensor

    d. Barometer

174. **What is the function of a gyroscope in a smart device?**

    a. Measuring speed

    b. Detecting magnetic fields

    c. Sensing orientation

    d. Capturing images

175. **Which technology is used by smart sensors to connect to the Internet?**

    a. DNS

    b. VPN

    c. Wi-Fi

    d. TCP/IP

176. **Which of the following sensors is used to measure atmospheric pressure?**

    a. Gyroscope

    b. Barometer

    c. Thermistor

    d. Magnetometer

177. **What is the purpose of a magnetometer in IoT devices?**

    a. Measuring temperature

    b. Sensing magnetic fields

    c. Capturing images

    d. Measuring humidity

178. **Which type of sensor is used to detect gases and pollutants in the air?**

    a. Gyroscope

    b. Gas sensor

    c. Proximity sensor

    d. Accelerometer

179. **What is the primary use of a photodetector in IoT applications?**

    a. Detecting sound

    b. Measuring temperature

    c. Sensing light

    d. Measuring pressure

180. **Which of the following sensors is used to measure force or weight?**

    a. Temperature sensor

    b. Force sensor

    c. Magnetometer

    d. Hygrometer

181. **In IoT, what is the main purpose of a soil moisture sensor?**

    a. Measuring air quality

    b. Detecting motion

    c. Monitoring soil moisture levels

    d. Measuring light intensity

182. **Which sensor is commonly used in smartphones to detect the phone's orientation?**

    a. Gyroscope

    b. Barometer

    c. Photodetector

    d. Thermistor

183. **What is the primary function of a pressure sensor in IoT applications?**

    a. Measuring speed

    b. Sensing orientation

    c. Measuring atmospheric pressure

    d. Detecting light intensity

184. **Which type of sensor is used in IoT devices to detect the presence of water?**

    a. Proximity sensor

    b. Water sensor

    c. Gas sensor

    d. Accelerometer

185. **What type of sensor is used to measure the flow rate of liquids or gases?**

    a. Temperature sensor

    b. Flow sensor

    c. Proximity sensor

    d. Hygrometer

186. **Which sensor technology is used for capturing images and video?**

    a. Lidar

    b. Camera sensor

    c. Gyroscope

    d. Pressure sensor

187. **Which of the following is an example of a wearable sensor in IoT?**

    a. Gas sensor

    b. Soil moisture sensor

    c. Fitness tracker

    d. Temperature sensor

188. **What is the purpose of a thermistor in IoT applications?**

    a. Detecting motion

    b. Measuring temperature

    c. Sensing magnetic fields

    d. Measuring light intensity

189. **Which of the following is not a common use of smart sensors in IoT?**

    a. Data acquisition

    b. Data processing

    c. Data storage

    d. Data destruction

190. **Which sensor is used to detect the presence of a magnetic field?**

    a. Thermistor

    b. Magnetometer

    c. Barometer

    d. Hygrometer

191. **Which sensor technology is used for indoor navigation in smart buildings?**

    a. Lidar

    b. RFID

    c. Gyroscope

    d. Thermistor

192. **What is a key advantage of using smart sensors in industrial IoT applications?**

    a. Reduced data accuracy

    b. Increased data latency

    c. Real-time monitoring

    d. Limited connectivity

193. **Which type of sensor is commonly used to measure temperature?**

    a. Gyroscope

    b. Thermocouple

    c. Accelerometer

    d. Magnetometer

194. **What type of sensor is used to detect the presence of gases such as CO2 or methane?**

    a. Humidity sensor

    b. Gas sensor

    c. Proximity sensor

    d. Light sensor

195. **In smart agriculture, what type of sensor would be used to monitor soil moisture levels?**

    a. Pressure sensor

    b. Soil moisture sensor

    c. Ultrasonic sensor

    d. Light sensor

196. **Which sensor is often used in smart homes to detect the opening or closing of doors and windows?**

    a. PIR sensor

    b. Contact sensor

    c. Accelerometer

    d. Gas sensor

197. **Which sensor would you use to measure air quality and particulate matter in a smart city?**

    a. CO2 sensor

    b. PM2.5 sensor

 c. Humidity sensor

 d. Light sensor

198. **To monitor rainfall in a smart weather station, which type of sensor is utilized?**

 a. Rain gauge sensor

 b. Ultrasonic sensor

 c. Barometer

 d. Anemometer

199. **Which sensor is used in a smart greenhouse to monitor the levels of sunlight?**

 a. Light sensor

 b. Humidity sensor

 c. Soil moisture sensor

 d. Temperature sensor

200. **To track and measure the level of noise pollution, which sensor is appropriate?**

 a. Sound sensor

 b. Vibration sensor

 c. Temperature sensor

 d. Proximity sensor

201. **What sensor is typically used to detect the concentration of ozone in the atmosphere?**

 a. Ozone sensor

 b. Gas sensor

 c. PM2.5 sensor

 d. Humidity sensor

202. **In a factory setting, which sensor would be used to monitor the speed of rotating machinery?**

 a. Proximity sensor

 b. Vibration sensor

 c. Accelerometer

 d. Pressure sensor

203. **Which type of sensor is essential for monitoring the temperature of industrial ovens or furnaces?**

   a. Thermocouple

   b. Gas sensor

   c. Pressure sensor

   d. Humidity sensor

204. **To measure the level of liquids in tanks, which sensor is most suitable?**

   a. Capacitive level sensor

   b. Ultrasonic level sensor

   c. Optical sensor

   d. Pressure sensor

205. **Which sensor is used to detect and measure vibrations in a structural health monitoring system?**

   a. Accelerometer

   b. Gas sensor

   c. Humidity sensor

   d. Proximity sensor

206. **To monitor the flow rate of liquids in pipes, which type of sensor is typically used?**

   a. Flow meter

   b. Pressure sensor

   c. Temperature sensor

   d. Vibration sensor

207. **Which sensor can be used to automatically control lighting based on the presence of occupants?**

   a. PIR sensor

   b. Temperature sensor

   c. Humidity sensor

   d. Gas sensor

208. **In smart home systems, which sensor is used for detecting smoke and fire?**

   a. Smoke detector

   b. Gas sensor

c. Temperature sensor

d. CO2 sensor

209. **Which sensor in a smart home would help in monitoring indoor air quality and humidity?**

   a. Humidity sensor

   b. Motion sensor

   c. CO2 sensor

   d. Light sensor

210. **To automate the irrigation system in a smart garden, which sensor would you use?**

   a. Soil moisture sensor

   b. Temperature sensor

   c. Light sensor

   d. CO2 sensor

211. **Which sensor is commonly used in smart security systems to detect unauthorized entry?**

   a. Contact sensor

   b. Gas sensor

   c. Temperature sensor

   d. Light sensor

212. **Which sensor is used to monitor blood glucose levels in diabetic patients?**

   a. Glucometer sensor

   b. Pulse oximeter

   c. ECG sensor

   d. Temperature sensor

213. **What type of sensor is used in continuous glucose monitoring systems?**

   a. Electrochemical sensor

   b. Infrared sensor

   c. Ultrasonic sensor

   d. Temperature sensor

214. **Which sensor is employed to measure blood pressure in a wearable health device?**

    a. Pressure sensor

    b. ECG sensor

    c. Pulse oximeter

    d. Accelerometer

215. **In remote health monitoring systems, which sensor would track a patient's physical activity levels?**

    a. Accelerometer

    b. Temperature sensor

    c. Pulse oximeter

    d. ECG sensor

216. **Which sensor is used to monitor and detect irregularities in heart rhythms?**

    a. ECG sensor

    b. Blood pressure sensor

    c. Pulse oximeter

    d. Glucometer sensor

217. **Which sensor is critical for monitoring the air pressure in car tires?**

    a. Tire pressure sensor

    b. Speed sensor

    c. Proximity sensor

    d. Temperature sensor

218. **To measure the distance between a vehicle and obstacles while parking, which sensor is used?**

    a. Ultrasonic sensor

    b. Gyroscope

    c. Magnetometer

    d. Pressure sensor

219. **Which sensor is utilized for detecting lane departures in modern vehicles?**

    a. Camera-based sensor

    b. Accelerometer

    c. Proximity sensor

    d. Temperature sensor

220. **What sensor is used to measure the engine temperature in automotive systems?**

    a. Thermocouple

    b. Gas sensor

    c. Pressure sensor

    d. Humidity sensor

221. **Which sensor monitors the vehicle's speed?**

    a. Speed sensor

    b. Proximity sensor

    c. Gyroscope

    d. Magnetometer

222. **Which sensor is used to monitor traffic congestion and vehicle flow in smart cities?**

    a. Inductive loop sensor

    b. Light sensor

    c. Gas sensor

    d. Temperature sensor

223. **To measure the level of water in reservoirs and rivers, which sensor is commonly used?**

    a. Ultrasonic level sensor

    b. Humidity sensor

    c. Temperature sensor

    d. Pressure sensor

224. **What sensor helps in detecting the presence and level of street lighting in smart cities?**

    a. Light sensor

    b. Humidity sensor

    c. Motion sensor

    d. Temperature sensor

225. **Which sensor is used to monitor and manage energy consumption in smart buildings?**

    a. Energy meter sensor

    b. Temperature sensor

    c. Gas sensor

    d. Humidity sensor

226. **To ensure efficient waste management in smart cities, which sensor is used in waste bins?**

    a. Ultrasonic level sensor

    b. Gas sensor

    c. Temperature sensor

    d. Proximity sensor

227. **Which sensor is used to monitor the growth of crops by measuring leaf wetness?**

    a. Leaf wetness sensor

    b. Soil moisture sensor

    c. Temperature sensor

    d. Light sensor

228. **To measure the ambient light levels for optimal crop growth, which sensor is used?**

    a. Light sensor

    b. Soil moisture sensor

    c. Temperature sensor

    d. Humidity sensor

229. **Which sensor helps in monitoring the nutrient levels in soil for precision farming?**

    a. Soil nutrient sensor

    b. Soil moisture sensor

    c. Temperature sensor

    d. Light sensor

230. **What sensor would be used to detect pests or diseases in crops?**

    a. Optical sensor

    b. Soil moisture sensor

    c. Gas sensor

    d. Humidity sensor

231. **Which sensor is used to measure the power consumption in an electrical grid?**

    a. Energy meter sensor

    b. Temperature sensor

    c. Voltage sensor

    d. Current sensor

232. To monitor and manage solar panel performance, which sensor would be used?

a. Irradiance sensor

b. Temperature sensor

c. Humidity sensor

d. Voltage sensor

233. What sensor is used to detect energy losses in electrical distribution systems?

a. Current sensor

b. Voltage sensor

c. Power sensor

d. Energy meter sensor

234. Which sensor helps in managing the battery health and status in energy storage systems?

a. Battery management system (BMS) sensor

b. Temperature sensor

c. Voltage sensor

d. Current sensor

235. Which sensor is employed to monitor the voltage levels in a smart grid?

a. Voltage sensor

b. Current sensor

c. Energy meter sensor

d. Power sensor

236. To measure and analyze current flow in electrical grids, which sensor is used?

a. Current sensor

b. Voltage sensor

c. Energy meter sensor

d. Power sensor

237. What sensor is used to detect faults and outages in smart grid systems?

a. Fault detection sensor

b. Voltage sensor

c. Current sensor

d. Temperature sensor

238. **Which sensor is used to measure the power factor in a smart grid?**

    a. Power factor sensor

    b. Voltage sensor

    c. Current sensor

    d. Energy meter sensor

239. **To ensure efficient energy distribution in smart grids, which sensor monitors load levels?**

    a. Load sensor

    b. Voltage sensor

    c. Current sensor

    d. Power sensor

240. **Which sensor is used to monitor the energy consumption of electrical devices in a building?**

    a. Energy meter sensor

    b. Voltage sensor

    c. Current sensor

    d. Temperature sensor

241. **To manage the lighting system based on ambient light conditions, which sensor is used?**

    a. Light sensor

    b. Temperature sensor

    c. Humidity sensor

    d. Motion sensor

242. **In smart transportation systems, which sensor is used for tracking vehicle locations via GPS?**

    a. GPS sensor

    b. Accelerometer

    c. Gyroscope

    d. Magnetometer

243. **Which sensor is used to monitor and manage the fuel levels in vehicles?**

    a. Fuel level sensor

    b. Temperature sensor

    c. Pressure sensor

    d. Gas sensor

244. **To ensure safety and stability in autonomous vehicles, which sensor is crucial for obstacle detection?**

    a. Lidar sensor

    b. Temperature sensor

    c. GPS sensor

    d. Gyroscope

245. **What sensor is used to monitor tire temperature in high-performance vehicles?**

    a. Tire temperature sensor

    b. Pressure sensor

    c. Speed sensor

    d. Fuel level sensor

246. **Which sensor helps in managing and analyzing traffic signal timings in smart cities?**

    a. Traffic camera sensor

    b. Light sensor

    c. Proximity sensor

    d. Temperature sensor

247. **Which sensor is commonly used for distance measurement in robotic systems?**

    a. Ultrasonic sensor

    b. Accelerometer

    c. Gyroscope

    d. Magnetometer

248. **In robotics, which sensor helps in detecting and managing the orientation of a robot?**

    a. Gyroscope

    b. Accelerometer

    c. Distance sensor

    d. Proximity sensor

249. **To detect and avoid obstacles in autonomous robots, which sensor is typically used?**

   a. Lidar sensor

   b. Ultrasonic sensor

   c. Camera sensor

   d. All of the above

250. **Which sensor is used in robotic arms to measure force and torque applied during operations?**

   a. Force sensor

   b. Distance sensor

   c. Temperature sensor

   d. Light sensor

251. **What sensor is used for tracking the position and movement of robotic systems?**

   a. Encoder sensor

   b. Temperature sensor

   c. Pressure sensor

   d. Light sensor

252. **In aerospace applications, which sensor is used to monitor atmospheric pressure at high altitudes?**

   a. Barometric pressure sensor

   b. Temperature sensor

   c. GPS sensor

   d. Humidity sensor

253. **Which sensor helps in measuring the altitude of an aircraft?**

   a. Altimeter sensor

   b. Gyroscope

   c. Accelerometer

   d. Magnetometer

254. **To monitor the structural health of spacecraft, which sensor is used?**

   a. Strain gauge sensor

   b. Temperature sensor

   c. Pressure sensor

   d. Humidity sensor

255. **Which sensor is used to track and manage the orientation and movement of satellites?**

   a. Star tracker sensor

   b. Accelerometer

   c. Gyroscope

   d. Altimeter

256. **What sensor is used to measure the radiation levels in space missions?**

   a. Radiation sensor

   b. Temperature sensor

   c. Pressure sensor

   d. Humidity sensor

Join our Discord space

Join our Discord workspace for latest updates, offers, tech happenings around the world, new releases, and sessions with the authors:

https://discord.bpbonline.com

Answers

Q.No.	Answers	Q.No.	Answers	Q.No.	Answers	Q.No.	Answers	Q.No.	Answers
1	c	31	b	61	d	91	c	121	c
2	a	32	b	62	d	92	b	122	c
3	d	33	c	63	b	93	b	123	c
4	b	34	d	64	b	94	c	124	c
5	b	35	b	65	d	95	c	125	c
6	a	36	b	66	c	96	b	126	a
7	d	37	a	67	a	97	b	127	c
8	c	38	d	68	a	98	c	128	a
9	d	39	b	69	b	99	b	129	a
10	c	40	b	70	b	100	b	130	b
11	c	41	c	71	d	101	a	131	a
12	d	42	b	72	d	102	b	132	b
13	c	43	b	73	b	103	b	133	c
14	d	44	a	74	b	104	b	134	c
15	a	45	d	75	b	105	b	135	c
16	c	46	b	76	b	106	b	136	d
17	d	47	b	77	d	107	b	137	a
18	b	48	c	78	d	108	b	138	b
19	d	49	b	79	b	109	c	139	a
20	c	50	b	80	b	110	b	140	b
21	b	51	b	81	b	111	c	141	c
22	c	52	b	82	b	112	b	142	a
23	d	53	b	83	c	113	b	143	d
24	c	54	b	84	b	114	d	144	b
25	d	55	b	85	b	115	b	145	b
26	c	56	b	86	b	116	c	146	b
27	d	57	a	87	c	117	b	147	c
28	b	58	b	88	b	118	a	148	b
29	c	59	b	89	b	119	c	149	d
30	d	60	b	90	a	120	a	150	b

Q.No.	Answers	Q.No.	Answers	Q.No.	Answers	Q.No.	Answers	Q.No.	Answers
151	a	173	c	195	b	217	a	239	a
152	b	174	c	196	b	218	a	240	a
153	c	175	c	197	b	219	a	241	a
154	c	176	b	198	a	220	a	242	a
155	b	177	b	199	a	221	a	243	a
156	a	178	b	200	a	222	a	244	a
157	b	179	c	201	a	223	a	245	a
158	b	180	b	202	b	224	a	246	a
159	c	181	c	203	a	225	a	247	a
160	b	182	a	204	b	226	a	248	a
161	c	183	c	205	a	227	a	249	d
162	d	184	b	206	a	228	a	250	a
163	b	185	b	207	a	229	a	251	a
164	c	186	b	208	a	230	a	252	a
165	b	187	c	209	a	231	a	253	a
166	b	188	b	210	a	232	a	254	a
167	a	189	d	211	a	233	d	255	a
168	b	190	b	212	a	234	a	256	a
169	b	191	b	213	a	235	a		
170	c	192	c	214	a	236	a		
171	b	193	b	215	a	237	a		
172	d	194	b	216	a	238	a		

Join our Discord space

Join our Discord workspace for latest updates, offers, tech happenings around the world, new releases, and sessions with the authors:

https://discord.bpbonline.com

CHAPTER 5
IoT Applications

Introduction

The **Internet of Things (IoT)** is changing how we interact with the world. IoT links common devices to the internet, creating new possibilities and applications across industries. This thorough guide covers some of IoT's most notable applications:

- **Smart homes**:
  - Home automation lets you manage lights, heating, and cooling remotely.
  - Smartphones can operate smart cameras, door locks, and alarm systems.
  - Compatible with Alexa and Google Home.

- **Healthcare**:
  - Wearable vital sign monitors for remote health monitoring.
  - Fall detection for seniors.
  - Smart pill bottles that remind patients to take.

- **Agriculture**:
  - Precision farming utilizes drones and sensors for crop health.
  - Automatic agricultural irrigation.

- Farm animal health and location monitoring.

- **Smart cities**:
  - Intelligent traffic management reduces congestion.
  - Waste management solutions for trash collection optimization.
  - Street lighting that saves energy.

- **Retail**:
  - Weight sensors on smart shelves may provide RFID data to the inventory system.
  - Beacon-based contextual advertising for customized shopping.
  - Automated checkout.

- **Transport and logistics**:
  - Tracking and scheduling fleet maintenance in real time.
  - Advanced driving assistance and predictive maintenance in connected autos.
  - Smart parking guides cars to available places.

- **Industrial IoT**:
  - Machine failure prediction from predictive maintenance.
  - Real-time equipment and system monitoring improves safety and efficiency.
  - Multi-location remote asset tracking.

- **Wearables**:
  - Fitbits and Apple Watches track health.
  - Enhanced real-world experiences using AR headsets.
  - Smart eyewear for hands-free industrial work.

- **Manage energy**:
  - Distributing energy efficiently and instantly using smart grids.
  - Remote solar and wind turbine monitoring.
  - Smart thermostats and appliances control household energy.

- **Environmental monitoring**:
  - Earthquake and tsunami sensors that alert people.
  - Air and water quality monitoring.
  - Forest fire detection.

Multiple choice questions

1. **Which of the following is an example of an application of IoT in the healthcare industry?**

   a. Weather forecasting

   b. Online gaming

   c. Smart agriculture

   d. Remote patient monitoring

2. **What is a common application of IoT in the transportation sector?**

   a. Virtual reality gaming

   b. Food delivery services

   c. Smart thermostats

   d. Vehicle tracking and fleet management

3. **Which industry benefits from IoT applications for optimizing energy consumption in buildings and homes?**

   a. Entertainment

   b. Retail

   c. Education

   d. Smart building automation

4. **How does IoT contribute to the field of agriculture?**

   a. By predicting sports events

   b. By monitoring fashion trends

   c. By enabling precision farming and smart irrigation

   d. By analyzing stock market trends

5. **What is a typical use case of IoT in the automotive industry?**

   a. Cooking recipes

   b. Fitness tracking

   c. Autonomous vehicles and vehicle-to-vehicle communication

   d. Social media networking

6. **Which of the following is a practical application of IoT in the retail sector?**

    a. Monitoring earthquakes

    b. Virtual reality gaming

    c. Smart shelves and inventory management

    d. Analyzing astronomy data

7. **How does IoT contribute to the field of environmental monitoring and conservation?**

    a. By predicting movie box office revenues

    b. By tracking social media trends

    c. By monitoring air and water quality, as well as wildlife habitats

    d. By analyzing culinary preferences

8. **Which sector benefits from IoT applications for optimizing supply chain operations and logistics?**

    a. Music industry

    b. Sports equipment manufacturing

    c. Fashion industry

    d. Logistics and shipping

9. **What is an example of an IoT application in the field of energy management?**

    a. Predicting the outcome of political elections

    b. Monitoring space exploration missions

    c. Smart metering and grid monitoring

    d. Analyzing historical art trends

10. **How does IoT contribute to the field of smart cities?**

    a. By predicting weather patterns

    b. By simulating online multiplayer games

    c. By optimizing movie production schedules

    d. By enhancing urban infrastructure and services

11. **What is a common application of IoT in the industrial sector (Industry 4.0)?**

    a. Monitoring pet care products

    b. Managing online food delivery services

    c. Industrial automation and predictive maintenance

    d. Analyzing social media engagement metrics

12. **Which sector benefits from IoT applications for improving waste management and recycling processes?**

    a. Recording studio equipment manufacturing

    b. Coffee shop chains

    c. Waste management and recycling companies

    d. Analyzing historical fashion trends

13. **How does IoT contribute to the field of home automation and smart living?**

    a. By predicting stock market trends

    b. By tracking online shopping trends

    c. By optimizing online advertising campaigns

    d. By controlling lighting, temperature, and appliances remotely

14. **What is the practical application of IoT in water management?**

    a. Predicting earthquakes

    b. Managing online music streaming platforms

    c. Smart irrigation systems and water quality monitoring

    d. Analyzing historical culinary trends

15. **Which sector benefits from IoT applications for enhancing customer experience and personalization?**

    a. Construction industry

    b. Book publishing

    c. Hospitality and tourism

    d. Space exploration

16. **What is an example of an IoT application in asset tracking and management?**

    a. Predicting weather forecasts

    b. Monitoring online fashion trends

    c. Tracking the location and condition of goods in supply chains

    d. Analyzing historical music trends

17. **How does IoT contribute to the field of wearable technology?**

    a. By predicting economic trends

    b. By monitoring stock market performance

    c. By analyzing historical movie trends

    d. By tracking health and fitness metrics

18. **What is a common application of IoT in smart agriculture?**

    a. Predicting traffic congestion

    b. Monitoring online gaming trends

    c. Precision farming and livestock monitoring

    d. Analyzing historical sports trends

19. **Which sector benefits from IoT applications for optimizing inventory and supply chain management?**

    a. Home decor industry

    b. E-commerce and online shopping

    c. Film production studios

    d. Online dating platforms

20. **How does IoT contribute to the health and wellness field?**

    a. By predicting fashion trends

    b. By monitoring political election outcomes

    c. By analyzing space exploration data

    d. By enabling remote health monitoring and fitness tracking

21. **What is the practical application of IoT in public safety and security?**

    a. Predicting social media trends

    b. Analyzing historical art trends

    c. Smart surveillance systems and disaster management

    d. Monitoring traffic patterns

22. **Which sector benefits from IoT applications for improving vehicle performance and maintenance?**

    a. Makeup and cosmetics industry

    b. Athletic footwear manufacturing

    c. Automotive industry and fleet management

    d. Historical literature analysis

23. **What is an example of an IoT application in entertainment and media?**

    a. Predicting educational trends

    b. Analyzing historical weather patterns

    c. Smart advertising and content delivery

    d. Monitoring real estate prices

24. **How does IoT contribute to the field of education?**

    a. By predicting fashion trends

    b. By monitoring political election outcomes

    c. By analyzing historical music trends

    d. By enabling remote learning and personalized education

25. **What is a typical application of IoT in environmental monitoring?**

    a. Predicting stock market trends

    b. Analyzing historical culinary trends

    c. Monitoring air quality, pollution levels, and climate change

    d. Tracking social media engagement

26. **Which sector benefits from IoT applications for optimizing energy consumption in homes and buildings?**

    a. Film production industry

    b. Electronic gadget manufacturing

    c. Home automation and energy management

    d. Historical fashion analysis

27. **How does IoT contribute to sports and fitness?**

    a. By predicting economic trends

    b. By monitoring historical literature trends

    c. By analyzing space exploration data

    d. By tracking athletic performance and health metrics

28. **What is the practical application of IoT in innovative water management?**

    a. Predicting traffic congestion

    b. Analyzing historical art trends

    c. Monitoring water supply, quality, and distribution

    d. Tracking social media engagement

29. **Which sector benefits from IoT applications for improving customer engagement and shopping experiences?**

    a. Construction equipment manufacturing

    b. Fine arts industry

    c. Retail and e-commerce

    d. Space exploration missions

30. How does IoT contribute to elderly care and assisted living?

    a. By predicting fashion trends

    b. By analyzing stock market performance

    c. By monitoring social media trends

    d. By enabling remote health monitoring and emergency response

31. What is a typical application of IoT in smart cities?

    a. Predicting weather forecasts

    b. Analyzing historical literature trends

    c. Urban infrastructure optimization and citizen services

    d. Tracking online shopping trends

32. Which sector benefits from IoT applications for improving manufacturing processes and quality control?

    a. Floral arrangement industry

    b. Online dating platforms

    c. Manufacturing and industrial automation

    d. Analyzing historical music trends

33. What is an example of an IoT application in financial services?

    a. Predicting traffic congestion

    b. Monitoring political election outcomes

    c. Smart banking and payment systems

    d. Analyzing historical sports trends

34. How does IoT contribute to the field of environmental sustainability?

    a. By predicting movie box office revenues

    b. By tracking online shopping trends

    c. By analyzing space exploration data

    d. By monitoring energy consumption and waste reduction

35. What is the practical application of IoT in asset management?

    a. Predicting earthquakes

    b. Monitoring historical literature trends

    c. Tracking the location and condition of equipment and assets

    d. Analyzing fashion trends

36. **Which sector benefits from IoT applications for optimizing patient care and medical treatment?**

    a. Culinary arts industry

    b. Online music streaming platforms

    c. Healthcare and medical facilities

    d. Historical literature analysis

37. **How does IoT contribute to energy efficiency and conservation?**

    a. By predicting social media trends

    b. By monitoring historical weather patterns

    c. By analyzing stock market performance

    d. By optimizing energy usage and reducing waste

38. **What is a common application of IoT in connected homes?**

    a. Predicting economic trends

    b. Monitoring online gaming trends

    c. Home automation and smart devices

    d. Analyzing historical art trends

39. **Which sector benefits from IoT applications for enhancing workplace safety and employee productivity?**

    a. Music composition industry

    b. Historical literature analysis

    c. Industrial and manufacturing sectors

    d. Online food delivery services

40. **How does IoT contribute to personal safety and security?**

    a. By predicting movie box office revenues

    b. By monitoring online shopping trends

    c. By analyzing historical music trends

    d. By enabling wearable devices for emergency response

41. **What is an example of an IoT application in smart retail?**

    a. Predicting traffic patterns

    b. Analyzing historical sports trends

    c. Smart shelves and inventory management

d. Monitoring air quality and pollution levels

42. **Which sector benefits from IoT applications for optimizing energy usage and reducing carbon footprint?**

    a. Online dating platforms

    b. Home decor and furnishings industry

    c. Oil and gas exploration

    d. Space exploration missions

43. **How does IoT contribute to wildlife conservation and biodiversity?**

    a. By predicting fashion trends

    b. By monitoring social media trends

    c. By analyzing historical literature trends

    d. By tracking animal behavior and habitat conditions

44. **What is the practical application of IoT in connected vehicles?**

    a. Predicting political election outcomes

    b. Monitoring stock market trends

    c. Vehicle diagnostics and remote control

    d. Analyzing historical culinary trends

45. **Which sector benefits from IoT applications for optimizing energy consumption and reducing operating costs?**

    a. Music recording studios

    b. Online gaming platforms

    c. Manufacturing and industrial automation

    d. Analyzing historical fashion trends

46. **How does IoT contribute to disaster management and emergency response?**

    a. By predicting economic trends

    b. By monitoring historical literature trends

    c. By analyzing stock market performance

    d. By enabling real-time monitoring and communication during disasters

47. **What is a typical application of IoT in connected consumer electronics?**

    a. Predicting social media trends

    b. Monitoring online shopping trends

   c. Home automation and smart devices

   d. Analyzing historical music trends

48. Which sector benefits from IoT applications for optimizing agricultural production and resource usage?

   a. Makeup and cosmetics industry

   b. Culinary arts industry

   c. Agriculture and agribusiness

   d. Historical literature analysis

49. How does IoT contribute to personalized marketing and customer engagement?

   a. By predicting movie box office revenues

   b. By tracking online shopping trends

   c. By analyzing historical art trends

   d. By delivering targeted advertisements and offers based on user behavior

50. What is an example of an IoT application in waste management and recycling?

   a. Predicting traffic patterns

   b. Analyzing historical sports trends

   c. Smart trash bins and recycling tracking

   d. Monitoring air quality and pollution levels

51. What is the practical application of IoT in smart lighting?

   a. Predicting fashion trends

   b. Monitoring political election outcomes

   c. Energy-efficient lighting and automated control

   d. Analyzing historical literature trends

52. Which sector benefits from IoT applications for enhancing agricultural productivity and crop management?

   a. Film production industry

   b. Online dating platforms

   c. Agriculture and precision farming

   d. Historical music analysis

53. **How does IoT affect air quality monitoring and pollution control?**

    a. By predicting economic trends

    b. By monitoring historical weather patterns

    c. By analyzing stock market performance

    d. By measuring pollutants and providing real-time alerts

54. **What is a typical application of IoT in connected appliances?**

    a. Predicting social media trends

    b. Monitoring online shopping trends

    c. Home automation and smart devices

    d. Analyzing historical culinary trends

55. **Which sector benefits from IoT applications for optimizing logistics and supply chain management?**

    a. Music composition industry

    b. Historical literature analysis

    c. Retail and e-commerce

    d. Online food delivery services

56. **How does IoT contribute to the field of wildlife monitoring and conservation?**

    a. By predicting movie box office revenues

    b. By tracking online shopping trends

    c. By analyzing space exploration data

    d. By using sensors to monitor animal behavior and habitats

57. **What is a practical application of IoT in the field of smart security systems?**

    a. Predicting traffic patterns

    b. Analyzing historical art trends

    c. Remote monitoring and automated security alerts

    d. Monitoring air quality and pollution levels

58. **Which sector benefits from IoT applications for improving patient care and medical diagnosis?**

    a. Music recording studios

    b. Online gaming platforms

    c. Healthcare and medical facilities

    d. Analyzing historical fashion trends

59. **How does IoT contribute to the field of waste reduction and sustainable practices?**

   a. By predicting fashion trends

   b. By monitoring social media trends

   c. By analyzing historical literature trends

   d. By optimizing resource usage and minimizing waste

60. **What is a common application of IoT in the field of connected appliances?**

   a. Predicting political election outcomes

   b. Monitoring stock market trends

   c. Home automation and smart devices

   d. Analyzing historical music trends

61. **Which sector benefits from IoT applications for optimizing fleet management and transportation?**

   a. Culinary arts industry

   b. Automotive manufacturing

   c. Online dating platforms

   d. Historical literature analysis

62. **How does IoT contribute to the field of water conservation and management?**

   a. By predicting economic trends

   b. By monitoring historical weather patterns

   c. By analyzing stock market performance

   d. By monitoring water usage and detecting leaks

63. **What is a practical application of IoT in the field of smart energy grids?**

   a. Predicting movie box office revenues

   b. Analyzing historical sports trends

   c. Automated energy distribution and demand management

   d. Monitoring air quality and pollution levels

64. **Which sector benefits from IoT applications for improving workplace safety and efficiency?**

   a. Music composition industry

   b. Manufacturing and industrial sectors

   c. Retail and e-commerce

   d. Space exploration missions

65. How does IoT contribute to the field of remote monitoring and telemedicine?

   a. By predicting social media trends

   b. By tracking online shopping trends

   c. By analyzing historical literature trends

   d. By enabling virtual medical consultations and health monitoring

66. What is a common application of IoT in the field of connected wearable devices?

   a. Predicting traffic patterns

   b. Monitoring political election outcomes

   c. Fitness tracking and health monitoring

   d. Analyzing historical art trends

67. Which sector benefits from IoT applications for optimizing energy consumption and reducing environmental impact?

   a. Fine arts industry

   b. Home decor and furnishings

   c. Oil and gas exploration

   d. Space exploration missions

68. How does IoT contribute to the field of smart waste management and recycling?

   a. By predicting fashion trends

   b. By monitoring social media trends

   c. By analyzing historical literature trends

   d. By optimizing waste collection and recycling processes

69. What is a practical application of IoT in the field of smart agriculture?

   a. Predicting economic trends

   b. Analyzing historical sports trends

   c. Precision farming and crop monitoring

   d. Tracking online shopping trends

70. Which sector benefits from IoT applications for improving customer engagement and personalized experiences?

   a. Music recording studios

   b. Historical literature analysis

   c. Retail and e-commerce

   d. Online dating platforms

71. **How does IoT contribute to the field of disaster response and recovery?**

    a. By predicting movie box office revenues

    b. By monitoring online gaming trends

    c. By analyzing space exploration data

    d. By providing real-time data for emergency management

72. **What is a common application of IoT in the field of connected health devices?**

    a. Predicting traffic patterns

    b. Monitoring historical literature trends

    c. Remote health monitoring and wearable devices

    d. Analyzing historical music trends

73. **Which sector benefits from IoT applications for optimizing resource allocation and usage?**

    a. Makeup and cosmetics industry

    b. Historical literature analysis

    c. Manufacturing and industrial sectors

    d. Online food delivery services

74. **How does IoT contribute to the field of environmental conservation and preservation?**

    a. By predicting social media trends

    b. By monitoring historical weather patterns

    c. By analyzing stock market performance

    d. By monitoring wildlife habitats and ecosystems

75. **What is the practical application of IoT in connected appliances?**

    a. Predicting political election outcomes

    b. Monitoring stock market trends

    c. Home automation and smart devices

    d. Analyzing historical culinary trends

76. **Which sector benefits from IoT applications for optimizing supply chain visibility and traceability?**

    a. Music composition industry

    b. Historical literature analysis

    c. Retail and e-commerce

    d. Aerospace and aviation

77. **Which IoT device can enhance room service in smart hotels?**

    a. Smart speakers

    b. Motion sensors

    c. Smoke detectors

    d. GPS trackers

78. **What is the primary benefit of IoT-enabled energy management in hotels?**

    a. Increased Wi-Fi speed

    b. Optimized HVAC systems

    c. Improved guest reviews

    d. Reduced laundry costs

79. **Which sector benefits from IoT applications for enhancing agricultural productivity and crop management?**

    a. Film production industry

    b. Online dating platforms

    c. Agriculture and precision farming

    d. Historical music analysis

80. **IoT in hospitality is most commonly associated with:**

    a. Blockchain transactions

    b. Predictive maintenance

    c. Virtual reality tours

    d. Smart room automation

81. **What is the practical application of IoT in intelligent security systems?**

    a. Predicting traffic patterns

    b. Analyzing historical art trends

    c. Remote monitoring and automated security alerts

    d. Monitoring air quality and pollution levels

82. **Which sector benefits from IoT applications for improving patient care and medical diagnosis?**

    a. Music recording studios

    b. Online gaming platforms

    c. Healthcare and medical facilities

    d. Analyzing historical fashion trends

83. **How does IoT contribute to waste reduction and sustainable practices?**

    a. By predicting fashion trends

    b. By monitoring social media trends

    c. By analyzing historical literature trends

    d. By optimizing resource usage and minimizing waste

84. **Which protocol is widely used for IoT connectivity in hospitality?**

    a. HTTP

    b. MQTT

    c. FTP

    d. POP3

85. **Which sector benefits from IoT applications for optimizing logistics and supply chain management?**

    a. Music composition industry

    b. Historical literature analysis

    c. Retail and e-commerce

    d. Online food delivery services

86. **How does IoT contribute to wildlife monitoring and conservation?**

    a. By predicting movie box office revenues

    b. By tracking online shopping trends

    c. By analyzing space exploration data

    d. By using sensors to monitor animal behavior and habitats

87. **What is the practical application of IoT in smart security systems?**

    a. Predicting traffic patterns

    b. Analyzing historical art trends

    c. Remote monitoring and automated security alerts

    d. Monitoring air quality and pollution levels

88. **How does IoT improve the food and beverage service in hotels?**

    a. Real-time stock monitoring

    b. Automated room assignment

    c. Self-cleaning kitchens

    d. Virtual check-in kiosks

89. **What technology enables IoT devices to identify guest preferences?**
    a. RFID
    b. Machine learning
    c. NFC
    d. Blockchain

90. **IoT-enabled predictive maintenance in hotels helps:**
    a. Monitor guest satisfaction
    b. Reduce equipment downtime
    c. Manage room bookings
    d. Improve marketing campaigns

91. **Which IoT device is critical for improving guest safety in hotels?**
    a. Smart locks
    b. Wearable fitness trackers
    c. Wireless routers
    d. Smart TVs

92. **IoT in hospitality enhances guest personalization by:**
    a. Offering fixed service options
    b. Collecting and analyzing guest behavior data
    c. Limiting device connectivity
    d. Reducing room cleaning frequency

93. **Which sensor is commonly used in IoT-based lighting systems in hotels?**
    a. Pressure sensor
    b. Proximity sensor
    c. Light dependent resistor (LDR)
    d. Gyroscope

94. **IoT-enabled room control systems are typically integrated using:**
    a. Mobile apps
    b. Printed brochures
    c. Smart thermostats only
    d. Guest ID cards

95. **How does IoT help in waste management in hospitality?**

    a. Automatic trash bin monitoring

    b. Real-time guest feedback

    c. Paperless billing systems

    d. Smart room service alerts

96. **IoT improves staff efficiency in hotels by:**

    a. Monitoring social media trends

    b. Delivering automated alerts for tasks

    c. Limiting guest interaction

    d. Reducing staff count

97. **What role does IoT play in improving event management in hotels?**

    a. Tracking guest reviews

    b. Real-time occupancy monitoring

    c. Reducing energy costs

    d. Predicting food preferences

98. **Which of the following IoT applications focuses on guest convenience?**

    a. Digital signage

    b. Smart keyless entry

    c. Predictive maintenance systems

    d. Water quality monitoring

99. **IoT-enabled mobile room keys in hotels use:**

    a. Bluetooth technology

    b. Zigbee protocol

    c. Infrared communication

    d. Satellite connectivity

100. **IoT applications in hospitality often require:**

    a. High data accuracy

    b. Increased manual intervention

    c. Minimal data collection

    d. Reduced guest interaction

101. **Which of the following is an example of an IoT application in smart agriculture?**
    a. Automated financial transactions
    b. Predictive maintenance in factories
    c. Precision irrigation systems
    d. Remote health monitoring

102. **In smart cities, which IoT application is commonly used to manage and reduce energy consumption?**
    a. Smart meters
    b. Wearable health devices
    c. Industrial automation systems
    d. Connected vehicles

103. **Which IoT application helps in monitoring patient vitals in real-time in healthcare settings?**
    a. Smart thermostats
    b. Wearable health trackers
    c. Smart parking systems
    d. Home security cameras

104. **What is a key benefit of using IoT in manufacturing industries?**
    a. Enhanced customer service
    b. Improved product marketing
    c. Predictive maintenance of equipment
    d. Faster software updates

105. **Which IoT application can be used to track the location and condition of shipments in logistics?**
    a. Smart home devices
    b. GPS tracking systems
    c. Environmental monitoring sensors
    d. Smart kitchen appliances

106. **In the context of smart homes, which IoT device can be used for energy management?**
    a. Smart locks
    b. Smart refrigerators
    c. Smart thermostats
    d. Smart lighting

107. **What IoT application is utilized for monitoring water quality in smart water management systems?**

    a. Water level sensors

    b. Water pressure regulators

    c. Smart faucets

    d. Water quality sensors

108. **Which IoT application can improve traffic flow and reduce congestion in smart cities?**

    a. Smart street lights

    b. Wearable fitness trackers

    c. Automated financial systems

    d. Smart waste management

109. **In precision agriculture, which IoT technology helps in monitoring soil conditions?**

    a. Soil moisture sensors

    b. Weather forecasting systems

    c. Smart irrigation controllers

    d. Crop health sensors

110. **Which IoT application in smart homes can enhance security?**

    a. Smart ovens

    b. Smart smoke detectors

    c. Smart washing machines

    d. Smart coffee makers

111. **Which IoT device is used for real-time monitoring of industrial processes?**

    a. Smart thermostats

    b. Industrial sensors

    c. Smart TVs

    d. Fitness trackers

112. **What is a common IoT application for ensuring food safety in supply chains?**

    a. Temperature logging systems

    b. Smart kitchen appliances

    c. Wearable health monitors

    d. Smart refrigerators

113. **Which IoT technology is used in smart grids to enhance energy distribution?**

    a. Smart meters

    b. Environmental sensors

    c. Smart irrigation systems

    d. Smart locks

114. **In retail, which IoT application helps in managing inventory levels?**

    a. Smart displays

    b. RFID tags

    c. Smart shelves

    d. Digital price tags

115. **Which IoT device can help with monitoring air quality in smart cities?**

    a. Air quality sensors

    b. Traffic cameras

    c. Smart home assistants

    d. Energy meters

116. **What IoT application can assist in optimizing fleet management for transportation companies?**

    a. Vehicle tracking systems

    b. Smart parking meters

    c. Smart road signs

    d. Intelligent traffic signals

117. **In smart farming, which IoT solution can help in monitoring livestock health?**

    a. GPS collars

    b. Soil moisture sensors

    c. Weather stations

    d. Automated irrigation systems

118. **Which IoT application is designed to improve water conservation in urban areas?**

    a. Smart irrigation systems

    b. Smart home thermostats

    c. Automated waste collection

    d. Energy-efficient lighting

119. **What IoT device is commonly used for enhancing home entertainment experiences?**

    a. Smart speakers

    b. Smart locks

    c. Smart refrigerators

    d. Smart doorbells

120. **In a smart office environment, which IoT application can help in managing workspace occupancy?**

    a. Occupancy sensors

    b. Smart desks

    c. Digital meeting schedulers

    d. Automated coffee machines

121. **Which IoT application is used to improve patient adherence to medication schedules?**

    a. Smart pill dispensers

    b. Wearable fitness trackers

    c. Remote monitoring systems

    d. Telemedicine platforms

122. **In smart agriculture, which IoT device helps monitor and control livestock feed?**

    a. Smart feeders

    b. GPS tracking collars

    c. Soil nutrient sensors

    d. Weather stations

123. **Which IoT solution helps reduce energy consumption in commercial buildings?**

    a. Building management systems

    b. Smart locks

    c. Smart TVs

    d. Smart refrigerators

124. **What IoT technology is used to monitor structural health in bridges and buildings?**

    a. Structural health monitoring sensors

    b. Weather sensors

    c. GPS tracking systems

    d. Energy meters

125. **In the context of smart transportation, which IoT application helps in route optimization for delivery services?**
    a. GPS navigation systems
    b. Traffic cameras
    c. Automated toll collection systems
    d. Smart road signs

126. **Which IoT device is used to monitor soil moisture levels for agriculture?**
    a. Soil moisture sensors
    b. Crop health sensors
    c. Weather stations
    d. Water quality sensors

127. **In smart cities, which IoT application is used for efficient waste management?**
    a. Smart waste bins
    b. Smart street lights
    c. Environmental sensors
    d. Air quality monitors

128. **Which IoT technology can assist in monitoring and controlling energy usage in industrial settings?**
    a. Smart energy meters
    b. Automated manufacturing systems
    c. Wearable health monitors
    d. Smart parking systems

129. **What IoT application can help track the health of athletes during training sessions?**
    a. Wearable fitness trackers
    b. Smart water bottles
    c. GPS sports watches
    d. Smart scales

130. **Which IoT device is commonly used for monitoring air quality in indoor environments?**
    a. Indoor air quality sensors
    b. Smart home assistants
    c. Weather stations
    d. Smart thermostats

131. **What IoT application is used to automate and optimize home lighting based on occupancy and ambient light?**

    a. Smart lighting systems

    b. Smart thermostats

    c. Smart doorbells

    d. Smart locks

132. **Which IoT solution can enhance precision in inventory management for warehouses?**

    a. RFID inventory tracking

    b. Automated shelf management systems

    c. Smart pallet systems

    d. Inventory management software

133. **In the context of smart grids, what IoT device helps in detecting power outages?**

    a. Smart grid sensors

    b. Energy meters

    c. Automated switches

    d. Power line sensors

134. **Which IoT application is used to monitor and control the temperature of server rooms?**

    a. Temperature sensors

    b. Air conditioning systems

    c. Environmental control systems

    d. Humidity sensors

135. **What IoT technology can improve the efficiency of public transportation systems?**

    a. Real-time tracking systems

    b. Automated fare collection systems

    c. Smart ticketing systems

    d. All of the above

136. **Which IoT device can be used for monitoring the condition of perishable goods during transportation?**

    a. Temperature and humidity sensors

    b. GPS trackers

    c. RFID tags

    d. Vibration sensors

137. **In smart buildings, which IoT application is used to enhance security by monitoring access points?**

    a. Smart security cameras

    b. Smart locks

    c. Access control systems

    d. Intrusion detection systems

138. **Which IoT application can help in monitoring and controlling HVAC systems in large facilities?**

    a. Building management systems

    b. Smart thermostats

    c. Environmental control systems

    d. Energy management systems

139. **What IoT technology is used for remote monitoring of environmental conditions in remote areas?**

    a. Environmental sensors

    b. Satellite communication systems

    c. Drones

    d. Automated weather stations

140. **Which IoT application can assist in automating the process of managing and scheduling conference rooms?**

    a. Smart room scheduling systems

    b. Automated lighting systems

    c. Smart door locks

    d. Smart HVAC systems

141. **Which IoT application can be used to monitor and control the temperature of industrial ovens?**

    a. Temperature sensors

    b. Smart thermostats

    c. Industrial automation systems

    d. Environmental control systems

142. **In smart homes, which IoT device can help in managing home security by providing real-time alerts?**

    a. Smart doorbells

    b. Smart refrigerators

    c. Smart lighting systems

    d. Smart thermostats

143. **What IoT application can help in reducing energy consumption by optimizing heating and cooling systems in residential buildings?**

    a. Smart thermostats

    b. Energy meters

    c. Automated lighting systems

    d. Smart appliances

144. **Which IoT technology can be utilized to monitor the condition of machinery in manufacturing environments?**

    a. Predictive maintenance sensors

    b. Smart thermostats

    c. Wearable fitness trackers

    d. Environmental sensors

145. **In the context of smart agriculture, which IoT application is used for monitoring crop health and growth?**

    a. Crop health sensors

    b. Soil moisture sensors

    c. Weather stations

    d. Automated irrigation systems

146. **Which IoT device can assist in managing and controlling water usage in urban environments?**

    a. Smart water meters

    b. Automated irrigation systems

    c. Water quality sensors

    d. Smart faucets

147. **In logistics, which IoT application helps in managing warehouse operations and inventory?**

    a. Automated inventory management systems

    b. GPS tracking systems

    c. Environmental sensors

    d. Smart shelving units

148. **Which IoT technology is used for monitoring and optimizing the performance of renewable energy systems like solar panels?**

    a. Solar panel monitoring systems

    b. Energy management systems

    c. Environmental sensors

    d. Smart meters

149. **In smart cities, which IoT application helps in monitoring and managing public lighting systems?**

    a. Smart street lights

    b. Smart parking meters

    c. Environmental sensors

    d. Public transportation systems

150. **What IoT device is used to monitor the condition of infrastructure such as roads and bridges?**

    a. Structural health monitoring sensors

    b. Weather sensors

    c. Traffic cameras

    d. Environmental sensors

151. **Which IoT application can enhance the shopping experience by providing personalized recommendations based on customer behavior?**

    a. Smart retail analytics systems

    b. RFID tags

    c. Smart shelves

    d. Digital price tags

152. **In smart homes, which IoT technology can assist in managing energy consumption for appliances?**

    a. Smart plugs

    b. Smart thermostats

    c. Smart lighting systems

    d. Smart locks

153. **Which IoT application can help improve traffic management by providing real-time data on traffic flow?**

    a. Intelligent traffic management systems

    b. GPS navigation systems

    c. Automated toll collection systems

    d. Smart road signs

154. **What IoT device can assist in monitoring and managing the condition of commercial refrigeration units?**

    a. Temperature and humidity sensors

    b. Smart thermostats

    c. Environmental sensors

    d. Smart locks

155. **In the context of smart farming, which IoT technology helps in monitoring the growth and health of plants?**

    a. Crop monitoring systems

    b. Soil moisture sensors

    c. Weather stations

    d. Automated irrigation systems

156. **Which IoT application is used for tracking and managing fleet vehicles in real-time?**

    a. GPS tracking systems

    b. Smart parking meters

    c. Fleet management software

    d. Automated toll collection systems

157. **What IoT technology can be used to monitor the performance of HVAC systems in large commercial buildings?**

   a. Building management systems

   b. Smart thermostats

   c. Environmental sensors

   d. Automated lighting systems

158. **In smart agriculture, which IoT application can optimize the use of fertilizers?**

   a. Nutrient monitoring sensors

   b. Soil moisture sensors

   c. Weather stations

   d. Crop health sensors

159. **Which IoT device can be used for monitoring the usage and condition of public transportation vehicles?**

   a. Vehicle tracking systems

   b. GPS navigation systems

   c. Smart ticketing systems

   d. Intelligent traffic signals

160. **In the context of smart buildings, which IoT application helps in managing and controlling lighting based on occupancy?**

   a. Occupancy sensors

   b. Smart lighting systems

   c. Building management systems

   d. Smart thermostats

161. **Which IoT application can help track and manage energy consumption in residential solar power systems?**

   a. Solar energy monitoring systems

   b. Smart thermostats

   c. Energy management systems

   d. Smart water meters

162. **In smart agriculture, which IoT device helps in controlling irrigation systems based on real-time soil moisture data?**

   a. Automated irrigation controllers

   b. Soil moisture sensors

c. Weather stations

d. Crop health sensors

163. **What IoT technology is used for monitoring and optimizing traffic light timings in urban areas?**

a. Intelligent traffic management systems

b. GPS tracking systems

c. Smart road signs

d. Automated toll collection systems

164. **Which IoT application can assist in managing and optimizing the usage of conference rooms in an office setting?**

a. Smart room scheduling systems

b. Building management systems

c. Automated lighting systems

d. Smart thermostats

165. **What IoT device is used to monitor the conditions of sensitive electronic equipment in data centers?**

a. Environmental sensors

b. Temperature and humidity sensors

c. Smart thermostats

d. Air quality monitors

166. **In smart homes, which IoT technology can enhance convenience by automating routine tasks?**

a. Smart home assistants

b. Smart lighting systems

c. Smart locks

d. Smart appliances

167. **Which IoT application can improve the accuracy of weather forecasting in smart agriculture?**

a. Weather stations

b. Soil moisture sensors

c. Crop health sensors

d. Automated irrigation systems

168. **In the context of smart cities, which IoT solution helps in reducing energy consumption in street lighting?**

    a. Smart street lights

    b. Smart parking meters

    c. Intelligent traffic signals

    d. Environmental sensors

169. **Which IoT application is used for managing and monitoring the quality of indoor air in commercial buildings?**

    a. Indoor air quality sensors

    b. Smart thermostats

    c. Environmental control systems

    d. Smart lighting systems

170. **What IoT device can assist in tracking and managing livestock health and location in farming?**

    a. GPS collars

    b. Soil moisture sensors

    c. Automated feeding systems

    d. Weather stations

171. **Smart mirrors in hotels equipped with IoT provide:**

    a. Basic room details

    b. Personalized guest services

    c. Enhanced lighting control

    d. Room cleaning schedules

172. **In logistics, what IoT application helps in real-time monitoring of fleet performance and vehicle health?**

    a. Fleet management systems

    b. GPS tracking systems

    c. Automated toll collection systems

    d. Smart parking meters

173. **Which IoT application is used for optimizing water distribution and usage in urban water systems?**

    a. Smart water management systems

    b. Automated irrigation systems

c. Water quality sensors

d. Smart faucets

174. **What IoT device is used to monitor and control the conditions of perishable goods in cold storage?**

a. Temperature and humidity sensors

b. Smart thermostats

c. Environmental control systems

d. Smart locks

175. **In the context of smart agriculture, which IoT technology helps in monitoring pest and disease outbreaks?**

a. Pest monitoring systems

b. Crop health sensors

c. Soil moisture sensors

d. Weather stations

176. **Which IoT application can help in optimizing the performance and reliability of industrial machinery?**

a. Predictive maintenance systems

b. Smart energy meters

c. Environmental sensors

d. Automated manufacturing systems

177. **In smart buildings, which IoT technology helps in managing and controlling heating and cooling systems based on occupancy?**

a. Smart HVAC systems

b. Smart thermostats

c. Building management systems

d. Environmental sensors

178. **Which IoT application is used to monitor and manage the conditions of stored goods in warehouses?**

a. Environmental monitoring systems

b. Inventory management systems

c. RFID tracking systems

d. Automated shelving systems

179. **What IoT device can help in tracking and managing the usage of energy resources in smart grids?**

    a. Smart meters

    b. Energy management systems

    c. Automated switches

    d. Environmental sensors

180. **In the context of smart homes, which IoT technology can enhance security by monitoring access points and movement within the house?**

    a. Smart security systems

    b. Smart locks

    c. Smart lighting systems

    d. Smart doorbells

181. **Which IoT technology helps in monitoring and controlling the energy consumption of appliances in a smart home?**

    a. Smart plugs

    b. Smart thermostats

    c. Smart lighting systems

    d. Smart doorbells

182. **In smart cities, which IoT application helps in managing parking spaces and reducing congestion?**

    a. Smart parking systems

    b. Smart traffic signals

    c. Intelligent road signs

    d. Automated toll booths

183. **What IoT device is used to monitor the safety and efficiency of industrial processes in real-time?**

    a. Industrial sensors

    b. Environmental sensors

    c. Predictive maintenance systems

    d. Smart energy meters

184. **Which IoT application can assist in optimizing supply chain operations by tracking inventory levels and location?**

    a. RFID tracking systems

    b. GPS tracking systems

    c. Automated inventory management systems

    d. All of the above

185. **In smart agriculture, which IoT technology helps in monitoring livestock health and activity?**

    a. GPS collars and activity trackers

    b. Soil moisture sensors

    c. Crop health sensors

    d. Weather stations

186. **How can IoT enhance security in hotels?**

    a. By installing wireless routers

    b. By enabling real-time surveillance

    c. By limiting guest movement

    d. By automating room bookings

187. **What IoT device is used for real-time monitoring of air quality in outdoor environments?**

    a. Air quality sensors

    b. Environmental monitoring systems

    c. Traffic cameras

    d. Weather stations

188. **In the context of smart homes, which IoT technology can assist in controlling and managing home entertainment systems?**

    a. Smart home assistants

    b. Smart speakers

    c. Smart TVs

    d. Smart lighting systems

189. **Which IoT application helps in managing and optimizing water usage in agricultural fields?**

     a. Smart irrigation systems

     b. Soil moisture sensors

     c. Weather stations

     d. All of the above

190. **IoT-enabled inventory systems in hospitality use:**

     a. RFID tags for real-time tracking

     b. Cloud storage for direct access

     c. Mobile apps for manual entry

     d. Wi-Fi for enhanced speed

191. **In logistics, which IoT application is used to track the real-time location and condition of shipments?**

     a. GPS tracking systems

     b. Temperature and humidity sensors

     c. RFID tags

     d. All of the above

192. **Which IoT technology helps in improving indoor air quality by controlling HVAC systems based on real-time data?**

     a. Smart HVAC systems

     b. Environmental sensors

     c. Indoor air quality monitors

     d. Smart thermostats

193. **In smart agriculture, which IoT application helps in predicting crop yield and optimizing harvest schedules?**

     a. Crop monitoring systems

     b. Weather stations

     c. Soil nutrient sensors

     d. Automated irrigation systems

194. **What IoT device can assist in monitoring and managing energy usage in large commercial buildings?**

     a. Energy management systems

     b. Smart meters

   c. Building management systems

   d. All of the above

195. **Which IoT application helps in automating and optimizing the management of smart grids for power distribution?**

   a. Smart grid sensors

   b. Automated grid management systems

   c. Energy management systems

   d. All of the above

196. **In the context of smart cities, which IoT technology helps in monitoring and managing waste collection and disposal?**

   a. Smart waste bins

   b. Environmental sensors

   c. Automated collection systems

   d. All of the above

197. **What IoT device can assist in enhancing the safety and security of residential properties?**

   a. Smart security cameras

   b. Smart locks

   c. Smart doorbells

   d. All of the above

198. **Which IoT application is used to track and optimize the performance of commercial refrigeration units?**

   a. Temperature and humidity sensors

   b. Smart thermostats

   c. Environmental control systems

   d. All of the above

199. **In smart farming, which IoT technology assists in monitoring and controlling greenhouse conditions?**

   a. Greenhouse climate control systems

   b. Soil moisture sensors

   c. Crop health sensors

   d. Weather stations

200. **Which IoT device can help in automating the process of energy consumption management in residential buildings?**

    a. Smart energy meters

    b. Smart plugs

    c. Smart thermostats

    d. All of the above

201. **Which IoT application is used for monitoring the condition of power transformers in the energy sector?**

    a. Transformer health monitoring sensors

    b. Smart meters

    c. Energy management systems

    d. Automated grid management systems

202. **In smart homes, which IoT technology helps in controlling home appliances through voice commands?**

    a. Smart home assistants

    b. Smart plugs

    c. Smart thermostats

    d. Smart doorbells

203. **What IoT device is used to monitor and manage the condition of fish tanks in aquaculture?**

    a. Water quality sensors

    b. Temperature sensors

    c. pH sensors

    d. All of the above

204. **Which IoT technology assists in managing and optimizing energy use in electric vehicle charging stations?**

    a. Smart charging stations

    b. Energy management systems

    c. Smart meters

    d. All of the above

205. **In smart agriculture, which IoT application is used to monitor the health and growth of vines in vineyards?**

   a. Vineyard monitoring systems

   b. Soil moisture sensors

   c. Weather stations

   d. Automated irrigation systems

206. **Which IoT technology helps in tracking and managing the usage of water resources in large-scale irrigation systems?**

   a. Smart irrigation controllers

   b. Soil moisture sensors

   c. Weather stations

   d. Water quality sensors

207. **What IoT device can be used to monitor and optimize indoor lighting conditions based on natural light availability?**

   a. Smart lighting systems

   b. Light sensors

   c. Environmental sensors

   d. Smart blinds

208. **In the context of smart transportation, which IoT application is used to manage and monitor traffic congestion?**

   a. Intelligent traffic management systems

   b. GPS navigation systems

   c. Traffic cameras

   d. Smart road signs

209. **What is the role of IoT-based smart thermostats in hotels**

   a. Enhancing lighting systems

   b. Automating guest check-ins

   c. Reducing energy consumption by adjusting room temperatures

   d. Managing housekeeping schedules

210. **What IoT application can be used to track and manage the condition of construction equipment on job sites?**

    a. Equipment monitoring systems

    b. GPS tracking systems

    c. Environmental sensors

    d. Automated maintenance systems

211. **Which IoT device assists in monitoring and optimizing the performance of renewable energy sources like wind turbines?**

    a. Wind turbine monitoring systems

    b. Smart meters

    c. Environmental sensors

    d. Energy management systems

212. **In smart cities, which IoT application is used to manage and monitor the condition of public parks and green spaces?**

    a. Park management systems

    b. Environmental sensors

    c. Smart irrigation systems

    d. Smart waste bins

213. **What IoT technology can assist in automating and managing the water supply in urban environments?**

    a. Smart water management systems

    b. Automated irrigation systems

    c. Water quality sensors

    d. Smart faucets

214. **In smart agriculture, which IoT device is used for monitoring and controlling greenhouse environments?**

    a. Greenhouse climate control systems

    b. Soil moisture sensors

    c. Crop health sensors

    d. Weather stations

215. **Which IoT application can enhance the accuracy of environmental monitoring in remote locations?**

    a. Remote environmental sensors

    b. Satellite communication systems

    c. Drones

    d. Automated weather stations

216. **What IoT device can assist in monitoring and managing the safety and efficiency of water treatment plants?**

    a. Water quality sensors

    b. Temperature sensors

    c. Smart meters

    d. Automated control systems

217. **In smart homes, which IoT technology is used for controlling and optimizing home energy consumption based on real-time data?**

    a. Smart energy management systems

    b. Smart thermostats

    c. Smart plugs

    d. All of the above

218. **Which IoT application is used to monitor and manage the condition of agricultural machinery and equipment?**

    a. Equipment monitoring systems

    b. GPS tracking systems

    c. Predictive maintenance systems

    d. All of the above

219. **What IoT technology is used to monitor and optimize the performance of smart grids in energy distribution?**

    a. Smart grid sensors

    b. Energy management systems

    c. Automated grid management systems

    d. All of the above

220. **In the context of smart agriculture, which IoT application helps in managing and optimizing the use of fertilizers and pesticides?**

    a. Smart farming systems

    b. Soil nutrient sensors

    c. Pest monitoring systems

    d. All of the above

221. **Which IoT application can assist in monitoring and managing the quality of air in industrial environments?**

    a. Industrial air quality sensors

    b. Environmental control systems

    c. Smart HVAC systems

    d. Air filtration systems

222. **In smart agriculture, which IoT technology helps in tracking and managing the growth and health of crops?**

    a. Crop management systems

    b. Soil sensors

    c. Weather stations

    d. Automated irrigation systems

223. **What IoT device is used to monitor the real-time usage and condition of medical equipment in hospitals?**

    a. Medical equipment monitoring systems

    b. Patient tracking systems

    c. Environmental sensors

    d. Smart energy meters

224. **Which IoT technology assists in managing and controlling the lighting conditions in smart buildings?**

    a. Smart lighting systems

    b. Light sensors

    c. Automated dimmers

    d. All of the above

225. **In smart cities, which IoT application is used for real-time monitoring of public transportation systems?**

   a. Smart transit management systems

   b. GPS tracking systems

   c. Automated ticketing systems

   d. All of the above

226. **What IoT device can help in optimizing the energy efficiency of residential heating systems?**

   a. Smart thermostats

   b. Smart energy meters

   c. Smart plugs

   d. All of the above

227. **Which IoT technology is used to monitor the structural health and stability of large infrastructure like bridges?**

   a. Structural health monitoring sensors

   b. Environmental sensors

   c. Traffic cameras

   d. Weather stations

228. **In the context of smart homes, which IoT device can be used to manage and monitor home security systems?**

   a. Smart security cameras

   b. Smart locks

   c. Smart doorbells

   d. All of the above

229. **Which IoT application helps in tracking and optimizing the performance of renewable energy sources like solar panels?**

   a. Solar panel monitoring systems

   b. Energy management systems

   c. Smart meters

   d. All of the above

230. **What IoT technology can assist in managing and optimizing the operation of water supply systems in urban areas?**

    a. Smart water management systems

    b. Automated irrigation systems

    c. Water quality sensors

    d. All of the above

231. **In smart agriculture, which IoT application is used to monitor the weather conditions affecting crop growth?**

    a. Weather stations

    b. Soil moisture sensors

    c. Crop health sensors

    d. Automated irrigation systems

232. **Which IoT device helps in optimizing the usage of public waste bins by monitoring their fill levels?**

    a. Smart waste bins

    b. Environmental sensors

    c. Automated waste collection systems

    d. All of the above

233. **What IoT technology is used to manage and monitor the condition of commercial refrigeration units?**

    a. Temperature and humidity sensors

    b. Smart thermostats

    c. Environmental control systems

    d. All of the above

234. **In smart buildings, which IoT application is used to control and optimize energy usage for heating and cooling systems?**

    a. Building management systems

    b. Smart thermostats

    c. Smart HVAC systems

    d. All of the above

235. **Which IoT application is used to monitor the condition and performance of agricultural irrigation systems?**

    a. Smart irrigation controllers

    b. Soil moisture sensors

    c. Weather stations

    d. All of the above

236. **What IoT technology helps in managing and controlling the safety and efficiency of industrial processes?**

    a. Industrial sensors

    b. Predictive maintenance systems

    c. Environmental monitoring systems

    d. All of the above

237. **In the context of smart homes, which IoT device assists in managing and optimizing indoor climate conditions?**

    a. Smart thermostats

    b. Smart air purifiers

    c. Environmental sensors

    d. All of the above

238. **Which IoT application helps in tracking the location and condition of fleet vehicles for logistics operations?**

    a. GPS tracking systems

    b. Fleet management systems

    c. Vehicle telematics

    d. All of the above

239. **What IoT technology is used to monitor and manage energy consumption in smart grids?**

    a. Smart meters

    b. Energy management systems

    c. Smart grid sensors

    d. All of the above

240. **In smart agriculture, which IoT device helps in monitoring and controlling the nutrient levels in soil?**

    a. Soil nutrient sensors

    b. Soil moisture sensors

    c. Weather stations

    d. Automated irrigation systems

241. **Which IoT application helps in monitoring and controlling the performance of heating systems in large buildings?**

    a. Building management systems

    b. Smart thermostats

    c. HVAC control systems

    d. All of the above

242. **In smart cities, which IoT technology assists in monitoring and managing the energy consumption of street lighting?**

    a. Smart street lights

    b. Energy management systems

    c. Environmental sensors

    d. All of the above

243. **What IoT device can be used to optimize the performance of industrial cooling systems?**

    a. Temperature and humidity sensors

    b. Cooling system monitors

    c. Smart thermostats

    d. All of the above

244. **Which IoT technology is most suitable for tracking guest movements within a hotel property?**

    a. Zigbee

    b. GPS

    c. Bluetooth Low Energy (BLE)

    d. MQTT

245. **In smart homes, which IoT technology can enhance security by detecting unusual activity and sending alerts?**

    a. Smart security systems

    b. Motion detectors

    c. Smart cameras

    d. All of the above

246. **Which IoT application helps in managing and optimizing the performance of smart irrigation systems in agriculture?**

    a. Automated irrigation controllers

    b. Soil moisture sensors

    c. Weather stations

    d. All of the above

247. **What IoT technology is used to monitor and control the temperature of sensitive materials during transportation?**

    a. Temperature monitoring sensors

    b. GPS tracking systems

    c. Environmental control systems

    d. All of the above

248. **In the context of smart buildings, which IoT device helps in controlling and optimizing lighting based on occupancy?**

    a. Smart lighting systems

    b. Occupancy sensors

    c. Automated dimmers

    d. All of the above

249. **Which IoT application is used to track and manage the condition of medical equipment in clinics and hospitals?**

    a. Medical equipment monitoring systems

    b. Environmental sensors

    c. Patient tracking systems

    d. All of the above

250. What IoT technology assists in monitoring and managing water usage and quality in urban water supply systems?

    a. Smart water management systems

    b. Water quality sensors

    c. Automated control systems

    d. All of the above

251. In smart agriculture, which IoT device helps in monitoring and managing soil pH levels?

    a. Soil pH sensors

    b. Soil moisture sensors

    c. Weather stations

    d. Automated irrigation systems

252. Which IoT application can help in managing and optimizing the performance of solar energy systems?

    a. Solar panel monitoring systems

    b. Energy management systems

    c. Smart meters

    d. All of the above

253. IoT-based occupancy sensors in rooms help hotels to:

    a. Optimize cleaning schedules

    b. Provide personalized room service

    c. Reduce booking errors

    d. Improve Wi-Fi connectivity

254. In smart homes, which IoT application can help in managing and optimizing home energy consumption?

    a. Smart energy management systems

    b. Smart plugs

    c. Smart thermostats

    d. All of the above

255. Which IoT device helps in tracking the location and condition of livestock in agriculture?

    a. GPS collars

    b. Health monitors

c. Activity trackers

d. All of the above

256. **What IoT technology assists in managing and controlling the performance of commercial HVAC systems?**

a. Building management systems

b. Smart thermostats

c. Environmental sensors

d. All of the above

257. **In smart cities, which IoT application is used to monitor and optimize public transportation routes and schedules?**

a. Smart transit management systems

b. GPS tracking systems

c. Automated ticketing systems

d. All of the above

258. **Which IoT technology is used to monitor and manage the safety and efficiency of water treatment processes?**

a. Water quality sensors

b. Smart meters

c. Automated control systems

d. All of the above

259. **What IoT device can help in tracking and managing the condition of refrigerated transport for perishable goods?**

a. Temperature and humidity sensors

b. GPS tracking systems

c. Environmental control systems

d. All of the above

260. **In the context of smart agriculture, which IoT application helps in monitoring and optimizing nutrient levels in soil?**

a. Soil nutrient sensors

b. Crop health monitoring systems

c. Automated irrigation systems

d. All of the above

261. **Which IoT technology is used for monitoring and managing the condition of energy storage systems like batteries?**

    a. Battery management systems

    b. Energy monitoring systems

    c. Smart meters

    d. All of the above

262. **In smart agriculture, which IoT device is used to monitor the health and growth of plants in greenhouses?**

    a. Greenhouse climate control systems

    b. Soil moisture sensors

    c. Crop health sensors

    d. All of the above

263. **What IoT technology assists in tracking and managing the condition of public infrastructure, like roads and bridges?**

    a. Structural health monitoring sensors

    b. Environmental sensors

    c. Traffic management systems

    d. All of the above

264. **Which IoT application helps in automating and managing the inventory levels in retail stores?**

    a. Smart inventory management systems

    b. RFID tags

    c. Barcode scanners

    d. All of the above

265. **In smart cities, which IoT device can be used to monitor and optimize energy usage in public buildings?**

    a. Energy management systems

    b. Smart meters

    c. Environmental sensors

    d. All of the above

266. **What IoT technology is used to manage and optimize the performance of water distribution systems in urban areas?**

    a. Smart water management systems

    b. Automated control systems

    c. Water quality sensors

    d. All of the above

267. **How does IoT improve spa and wellness services in hotels?**

    a. By automating therapy session bookings

    b. By monitoring water quality in pools and spas

    c. By managing temperature in gym areas

    d. All of the above

268. **Which IoT application is used to monitor and manage the health and productivity of dairy cattle in agriculture?**

    a. Livestock health monitoring systems

    b. GPS collars

    c. Activity trackers

    d. All of the above

269. **Which IoT application is commonly used for guest feedback collection in hotels?**

    a. Smart kiosks

    b. Chatbots

    c. NFC-enabled devices

    d. Voice-activated assistants

270. **In smart agriculture, which IoT application helps in monitoring the water usage efficiency of irrigation systems?**

    a. Smart irrigation controllers

    b. Soil moisture sensors

    c. Weather stations

    d. All of the above

271. **IoT-based digital signage in hospitality is primarily used for:**

    a. Advertising personalized offers to guests

    b. Monitoring room temperatures

    c. Automating reservations

    d. Energy consumption monitoring

272. **What IoT device helps in monitoring and managing the performance of renewable energy sources like wind turbines?**

    a. Wind turbine monitoring systems

    b. Smart meters

    c. Energy management systems

    d. All of the above

273. **In smart cities, which IoT application is used to monitor and optimize public waste management systems?**

    a. Smart waste bins

    b. Automated collection systems

    c. Environmental sensors

    d. All of the above

274. **Which IoT technology helps in tracking and managing the condition of refrigerated goods during transportation?**

    a. Temperature and humidity sensors

    b. GPS tracking systems

    c. Environmental control systems

    d. All of the above

275. **What IoT device can assist in monitoring and managing the safety of industrial equipment and processes?**

    a. Industrial sensors

    b. Predictive maintenance systems

    c. Environmental monitoring systems

    d. All of the above

276. **In smart agriculture, which IoT technology helps in managing and optimizing soil fertility and nutrient levels?**

    a. Soil nutrient sensors

    b. Crop health monitoring systems

    c. Automated irrigation systems

    d. All of the above

277. **Which IoT application assists in monitoring and managing energy consumption in large commercial buildings?**

    a. Smart energy management systems

    b. Smart meters

    c. Building management systems

    d. All of the above

278. **Predictive analytics in IoT hospitality applications use:**

    a. Historical guest data

    b. Real-time sensor inputs

    c. Machine learning algorithms

    d. All of the above

279. **In the context of smart homes, which IoT application helps in controlling and managing energy use for lighting?**

    a. Smart lighting systems

    b. Automated dimmers

    c. Light sensors

    d. All of the above

280. **Which IoT technology is used to monitor and manage the condition and performance of commercial refrigeration units?**

    a. Temperature and humidity sensors

    b. Smart thermostats

    c. Environmental control systems

    d. All of the above

281. **Which IoT device helps in monitoring the energy consumption and efficiency of residential solar panels?**

    a. Solar panel monitoring systems

    b. Energy management systems

    c. Smart meters

    d. All of the above

282. **In smart agriculture, which IoT technology assists in managing the irrigation of crops based on real-time weather data?**

    a. Smart irrigation systems

    b. Weather stations

    c. Soil moisture sensors

    d. All of the above

283. **Which IoT application is used to monitor and optimize the performance of industrial refrigeration systems?**

    a. Temperature monitoring systems

    b. Energy management systems

    c. Environmental control systems

    d. All of the above

284. **What IoT technology helps in managing and optimizing the safety and efficiency of large-scale water treatment facilities?**

    a. Water quality sensors

    b. Automated control systems

    c. Environmental monitoring systems

    d. All of the above

285. **In smart homes, which IoT device can assist in managing and optimizing energy use for heating and cooling?**

    a. Smart thermostats

    b. Smart HVAC systems

    c. Energy management systems

    d. All of the above

286. **Which IoT application helps in tracking and managing the location and condition of fleet vehicles in logistics?**

    a. GPS tracking systems

    b. Fleet management systems

    c. Vehicle telematics

    d. All of the above

287. **Smart hotel rooms use IoT devices for:**

    a. Controlling room temperature and lighting via mobile apps

    b. Automating front desk communications

c. Monitoring food delivery times

d. Managing conference room bookings

288. **In the context of smart agriculture, which IoT device is used to monitor the health and growth of livestock?**

a. GPS collars

b. Health monitors

c. Activity trackers

d. All of the above

289. **IoT-enabled concierge services in hotels are typically powered by:**

a. AI-driven chatbots and voice assistants

b. Blockchain technology

c. Smart thermostats

d. NFC-enabled locks

290. **What IoT technology is used to track and manage the condition of water distribution systems in smart cities?**

a. Smart water management systems

b. Automated control systems

c. Water quality sensors

d. All of the above

291. **In smart buildings, which IoT application helps in controlling and optimizing energy usage based on occupancy?**

a. Building management systems

b. Smart lighting systems

c. Smart thermostats

d. All of the above

292. **Which IoT device assists in monitoring and managing the condition of public waste bins in urban areas?**

a. Smart waste bins

b. Environmental sensors

c. Automated collection systems

d. All of the above

293. **What IoT technology is used to monitor and manage the condition of commercial air conditioning systems?**

   a. Smart thermostats

   b. HVAC control systems

   c. Environmental sensors

   d. All of the above

294. **In the context of smart agriculture, which IoT application helps in optimizing the use of fertilizers and pesticides?**

   a. Smart farming systems

   b. Soil nutrient sensors

   c. Pest monitoring systems

   d. All of the above

295. **Which IoT device is used for monitoring the health and safety of elderly individuals in a smart home environment?**

   a. Health monitoring systems

   b. Smart wearables

   c. Emergency alert systems

   d. All of the above

296. **IoT-based air quality sensors in hotels are primarily used to:**

   a. Maintain guest satisfaction by improving indoor air quality

   b. Track housekeeping schedules

   c. Analyze weather conditions

   d. Automate HVAC system repairs

297. **In smart cities, which IoT application is used to monitor and manage the condition of public parks and green spaces?**

   a. Park management systems

   b. Environmental sensors

   c. Smart irrigation systems

   d. All of the above

298. **Which IoT technology is used to track and manage the condition of refrigerated transport for perishable goods?**

    a. Temperature and humidity sensors

    b. GPS tracking systems

    c. Environmental control systems

    d. All of the above

299. **What IoT application helps in managing and optimizing the safety and performance of large-scale industrial equipment?**

    a. Predictive maintenance systems

    b. Industrial sensors

    c. Environmental monitoring systems

    d. All of the above

300. **In smart homes, which IoT device helps in controlling and managing the safety and efficiency of home appliances?**

    a. Smart plugs

    b. Smart appliances

    c. Home automation systems

    d. All of the above

Join our Discord space

Join our Discord workspace for latest updates, offers, tech happenings around the world, new releases, and sessions with the authors:

https://discord.bpbonline.com

Answers

Q.No.	Answers	Q.No.	Answers	Q.No.	Answers	Q.No.	Answers	Q.No.	Answers
1	d	31	c	61	b	91	c	121	a
2	d	32	c	62	d	92	d	122	a
3	d	33	c	63	c	93	c	123	a
4	c	34	d	64	b	94	c	124	a
5	c	35	c	65	d	95	d	125	a
6	c	36	c	66	c	96	c	126	a
7	c	37	d	67	b	97	c	127	a
8	d	38	c	68	d	98	d	128	a
9	c	39	c	69	c	99	c	129	a
10	d	40	d	70	c	100	c	130	a
11	c	41	c	71	d	101	c	131	a
12	c	42	b	72	c	102	a	132	a
13	d	43	d	73	c	103	b	133	a
14	c	44	c	74	d	104	c	134	a
15	c	45	c	75	c	105	b	135	d
16	c	46	d	76	c	106	c	136	a
17	d	47	c	77	d	107	d	137	c
18	c	48	c	78	c	108	a	138	a
19	b	49	d	79	c	109	a	139	a
20	d	50	c	80	d	110	b	140	a
21	c	51	c	81	c	111	b	141	a
22	c	52	c	82	c	112	a	142	a
23	c	53	d	83	d	113	a	143	a
24	d	54	c	84	c	114	b	144	a
25	c	55	c	85	c	115	a	145	a
26	c	56	d	86	d	116	a	146	a
27	d	57	c	87	c	117	a	147	a
28	c	58	c	88	c	118	a	148	a
29	c	59	d	89	d	119	a	149	a
30	d	60	c	90	c	120	a	150	a

Q.No.	Answers	Q.No.	Answers	Q.No.	Answers	Q.No.	Answers	Q.No.	Answers
151	a	181	a	211	a	241	d	271	d
152	a	182	a	212	a	242	a	272	a
153	a	183	a	213	a	243	a	273	d
154	a	184	d	214	a	244	d	274	a
155	a	185	a	215	a	245	d	275	d
156	a	186	d	216	a	246	d	276	a
157	a	187	a	217	d	247	a	277	d
158	a	188	a	218	d	248	d	278	d
159	a	189	d	219	d	249	a	279	d
160	a	190	a	220	d	250	d	280	a
161	a	191	d	221	a	251	a	281	d
162	a	192	a	222	a	252	d	282	d
163	a	193	a	223	a	253	a	283	a
164	a	194	d	224	d	254	d	284	d
165	b	195	d	225	d	255	d	285	d
166	a	196	d	226	a	256	d	286	d
167	a	197	d	227	a	257	d	287	a
168	a	198	a	228	d	258	d	288	d
169	a	199	a	229	d	259	a	289	d
170	a	200	d	230	a	260	a	290	d
171	a	201	a	231	a	261	a	291	d
172	a	202	a	232	a	262	d	292	a
173	a	203	d	233	a	263	a	293	d
174	a	204	d	234	d	264	a	294	d
175	a	205	a	235	d	265	d	295	d
176	a	206	a	236	d	266	d	296	d
177	a	207	a	237	d	267	d	297	d
178	a	208	a	238	d	268	d	298	a
179	a	209	a	239	d	269	d	299	d
180	a	210	a	240	a	270	d	300	d

CHAPTER 6
Interview Questions

Introduction

This chapter offers a concentrated examination of the primary topics and concepts associated with the **Internet of Things** (**IoT**) that are frequently highlighted in technical interviews. This chapter also endeavors to anticipate the types of inquiries that readers may encounter during interviews for positions associated with the IoT. It covers fundamental concepts, including devices, sensors, connectivity, and cloud computing, which together create an ecosystem that supports seamless communication. The primary characteristic of IoT devices is their ability to remain connected to the internet, thereby enabling real-time monitoring and control across multiple domains. This ecosystem is transforming industries such as healthcare, agriculture, transportation, energy, and waste management by improving efficiency, security, and decision-making. For instance, IoT enables remote patient monitoring in healthcare, precision farming in agriculture, predictive maintenance in industries, and smart traffic management in transportation. It also plays a crucial role in enhancing public safety, disaster management, environmental monitoring, and urban planning, thus supporting the concept of smart cities. With the integration of edge computing and cloud platforms, IoT systems are becoming more reliable, scalable, and secure. Moreover, the use of ML and predictive analytics in IoT data processing provides valuable insights that help forecast trends and optimize operations. Despite challenges such as privacy concerns, interoperability, and power consumption, IoT continues to revolutionize the modern world with innovative and sustainable solutions.

This chapter aims to provide readers with a comprehensive comprehension of the types of questions they may encounter during interviews for positions related to the IoT. The objective of this chapter is to address a wide range of subjects, such as the fundamental principles of IoT, industry-specific applications, problem-solving scenarios, and specific technical skills. The chapter assists readers in evaluating their knowledge, identifying voids, and reinforcing their comprehension of critical IoT concepts by presenting a diverse array of multiple-choice questions. Furthermore, it endeavors to offer readers a better understanding of the expectations and thought processes of interviewers, thereby allowing them to approach their interviews with confidence and clarity. In the final analysis, this chapter is intended to serve as a practical resource for prospective IoT professionals, assisting them in their preparation for successful interviews and career advancement within the IoT sector.

Multiple choice questions

1. **What does IoT stand for?**
    a. Internet of Technology
    b. Internet of Things
    c. Internet of Telecommunication
    d. Internet of Techniques

2. **Which of the following is not a component of the IoT ecosystem?**
    a. Devices
    b. Sensors
    c. Cloud computing
    d. Robots

3. **What is the primary characteristic of IoT devices?**
    a. To only collect data
    b. To process data locally
    c. To connect to the internet
    d. To replace traditional devices

4. **Which benefit of edge computing is most cited?**
    a. It improves device aesthetics
    b. It reduces the need for cloud computing
    c. It eliminates the need for sensors
    d. It enhances data security

5. **How does the IoT ecosystem contribute to improving healthcare services?**

   a. By increasing patient workload

   b. By enabling remote patient monitoring and personalized treatment

   c. By eliminating the need for doctors

   d. By promoting unnecessary medical procedures

6. **How does the IoT ecosystem contribute to enhancing agriculture precision?**

   a. By promoting excessive use of pesticides

   b. By enabling data-driven decision-making in farming practices

   c. By eliminating the need for irrigation

   d. By relying solely on traditional farming methods

7. **What is the potential benefit of implementing an IoT ecosystem in the industrial sector?**

   a. Increasing operational inefficiencies

   b. Reducing data collection and analysis

   c. Enabling predictive maintenance and real-time monitoring

   d. Eliminating the need for human workers

8. **How does the IoT ecosystem contribute to enhancing transportation systems?**

   a. By increasing traffic congestion

   b. By enabling real-time traffic monitoring and navigation

   c. By promoting higher fuel consumption

   d. By reducing the importance of public transportation

9. **How does the IoT ecosystem contribute to enhancing energy efficiency in buildings?**

   a. By increasing energy wastage

   b. By enabling real-time monitoring and optimization of energy usage

   c. By promoting excessive use of electrical devices

   d. By eliminating the need for energy conservation

10. **How does the IoT ecosystem contribute to improving waste management?**

    a. By increasing littering and waste generation

    b. By enabling real-time monitoring of waste levels and collection

    c. By discouraging waste recycling efforts

    d. By promoting landfill usage

11. **How does the IoT ecosystem contribute to enhancing environmental monitoring?**

   a. By promoting increased pollution

   b. By enabling real-time monitoring of air and water quality

   c. By encouraging deforestation

   d. By reducing the need for pollution control

12. **How does the IoT ecosystem contribute to enhancing disaster management?**

   a. By increasing the impact of disasters

   b. By enabling real-time monitoring and early warnings

   c. By promoting unsafe practices during disasters

   d. By reducing the need for emergency response

13. **How does the IoT ecosystem contribute to enhancing public safety and security?**

   a. By promoting criminal activities

   b. By enabling real-time surveillance and emergency response

   c. By increasing privacy breaches

   d. By eliminating the need for security measures

14. **How does the IoT ecosystem contribute to enhancing retail operations?**

   a. By increasing stock shortages and customer dissatisfaction

   b. By enabling real-time inventory management and personalized shopping experiences

   c. By discouraging online shopping

   d. By reducing the need for customer data collection

15. **How does the IoT ecosystem contribute to enhancing waste recycling?**

   a. By promoting improper waste disposal

   b. By enabling real-time monitoring of recycling bins

   c. By discouraging sustainable practices

   d. By increasing landfill usage

16. **How does the IoT ecosystem contribute to enhancing air quality monitoring?**

   a. By increasing air pollution

   b. By enabling real-time monitoring of pollutants and air quality indexes

   c. By promoting activities harmful to air quality

   d. By reducing the importance of clean air

17. **How does the IoT ecosystem contribute to enhancing disaster recovery and response?**

    a. By making disasters more destructive

    b. By enabling real-time communication and coordination during disasters

    c. By increasing response time and inefficiency

    d. By disregarding disaster management efforts

18. **How does the IoT ecosystem contribute to enhancing smart energy management?**

    a. By increasing energy wastage

    b. By enabling real-time monitoring and optimization of energy usage

    c. By ignoring energy conservation efforts

    d. By reducing the importance of renewable energy sources

19. **In what ways does the IoT ecosystem support and improve urban planning and smart city development?**

    a. By increasing urban sprawl and traffic congestion

    b. By enabling real-time monitoring of infrastructure and public services

    c. By discouraging sustainable development

    d. By limiting access to urban amenities

20. **How does the IoT ecosystem contribute to enhancing public safety and security?**

    a. By promoting criminal activities

    b. By enabling real-time surveillance and emergency response

    c. By increasing privacy breaches

    d. By eliminating the need for security measures

21. **How does the IoT ecosystem contribute to enhancing retail operations?**

    a. By increasing stock shortages and customer dissatisfaction

    b. By enabling real-time inventory management and personalized shopping experiences

    c. By discouraging online shopping

    d. By reducing the need for customer data collection

22. **How does the IoT ecosystem contribute to enhancing waste recycling?**

    a. By promoting improper waste disposal

    b. By enabling real-time monitoring of recycling bins

    c. By discouraging sustainable practices

    d. By increasing landfill usage

23. **How does the IoT ecosystem contribute to enhancing air quality monitoring?**
    a. By increasing air pollution
    b. By enabling real-time monitoring of pollutants and air quality indexes
    c. By promoting activities harmful to air quality
    d. By reducing the importance of clean air

24. **How does the IoT ecosystem contribute to enhancing disaster recovery and response?**
    a. By making disasters more destructive
    b. By enabling real-time communication and coordination during disasters
    c. By increasing response time and inefficiency
    d. By disregarding disaster management efforts

25. **How does the IoT ecosystem contribute to enhancing smart energy management?**
    a. By increasing energy wastage
    b. By enabling real-time monitoring and optimization of energy usage
    c. By ignoring energy conservation efforts
    d. By reducing the importance of renewable energy sources

26. **How does the IoT ecosystem contribute to enhancing urban planning?**
    a. By increasing urban sprawl and traffic congestion
    b. By enabling real-time monitoring of infrastructure and public services
    c. By discouraging sustainable development
    d. By limiting access to urban amenities

27. **In what way does the IoT ecosystem support public safety and security?**
    a. By encouraging unlawful behavior
    b. By providing real-time monitoring and faster emergency responses
    c. By exposing sensitive information to threats
    d. By removing the need for safety protocols

28. **How does the IoT ecosystem contribute to enhancing retail operations?**
    a. By increasing stock shortages and customer dissatisfaction
    b. By enabling real-time inventory management and personalized shopping experiences
    c. By discouraging online shopping
    d. By reducing the need for customer data collection

29. **How does the IoT ecosystem contribute to enhancing waste recycling?**

    a. By promoting improper waste disposal

    b. By enabling real-time monitoring of recycling bins

    c. By discouraging sustainable practices

    d. By increasing landfill usage

30. **How does the IoT ecosystem contribute to enhancing air quality monitoring?**

    a. By increasing air pollution

    b. By enabling real-time monitoring of pollutants and air quality indexes

    c. By promoting activities harmful to air quality

    d. By reducing the importance of clean air

31. **How does the IoT ecosystem contribute to enhancing disaster recovery and response?**

    a. By making disasters more destructive

    b. By enabling real-time communication and coordination during disasters

    c. By increasing response time and inefficiency

    d. By disregarding disaster management efforts

32. **How does the IoT ecosystem contribute to enhancing smart energy management?**

    a. By increasing energy wastage

    b. By enabling real-time monitoring and optimization of energy usage

    c. By ignoring energy conservation efforts

    d. By reducing the importance of renewable energy sources

33. **How does the IoT ecosystem contribute to enhancing urban planning?**

    a. By increasing urban sprawl and traffic congestion

    b. By enabling real-time monitoring of infrastructure and public services

    c. By discouraging sustainable development

    d. By limiting access to urban amenities

34. **How does the IoT ecosystem contribute to improving healthcare services?**

    a. By increasing patient wait times

    b. By enabling real-time patient monitoring and remote consultations

    c. By discouraging preventive healthcare measures

    d. By reducing the role of medical professionals

35. **How does the IoT ecosystem contribute to enhancing water management?**

    a. By increasing water wastage

    b. By enabling real-time monitoring of water levels and quality

    c. By promoting excessive water consumption

    d. By disregarding water conservation efforts

36. **How does the IoT ecosystem contribute to enhancing traffic management?**

    a. By increasing traffic congestion

    b. By enabling real-time traffic monitoring and optimization

    c. By promoting reckless driving

    d. By eliminating the need for traffic signals

37. **What is the potential impact of the IoT ecosystem on the environment?**

    a. Increasing pollution

    b. Reducing resource consumption

    c. Accelerating deforestation

    d. Worsening climate change

38. **How does the IoT ecosystem contribute to enhancing supply chain management?**

    a. By increasing supply chain disruptions

    b. By enabling real-time tracking of goods and inventory

    c. By promoting excessive production

    d. By reducing the need for logistical coordination

39. **How does the IoT ecosystem contribute to enhancing waste recycling?**

    a. By promoting improper waste disposal

    b. By enabling real-time monitoring of recycling bins

    c. By discouraging sustainable practices

    d. By increasing landfill usage

40. **Which approach allows smart buildings to reduce power consumption using IoT technology?**

    a. Wasting more electricity through automation

    b. Monitoring and optimizing energy use through connected sensors

    c. Encouraging overuse of appliances

    d. Ignoring the importance of saving energy

41. **How does the IoT ecosystem contribute to enhancing environmental monitoring?**

    a. By promoting increased pollution

    b. By enabling real-time monitoring of air and water quality

    c. By encouraging deforestation

    d. By reducing the need for pollution control

42. **How does the IoT ecosystem contribute to enhancing disaster recovery and response?**

    a. By making disasters more destructive

    b. By enabling real-time communication and coordination during disasters

    c. By increasing response time and inefficiency

    d. By disregarding disaster management efforts

43. **How does the IoT ecosystem contribute to enhancing smart energy management?**

    a. By increasing energy wastage

    b. By enabling real-time monitoring and optimization of energy usage

    c. By ignoring energy conservation efforts

    d. By reducing the importance of renewable energy sources

44. **How does the IoT ecosystem contribute to enhancing urban planning?**

    a. By increasing urban sprawl and traffic congestion

    b. By enabling real-time monitoring of infrastructure and public services

    c. By discouraging sustainable development

    d. By limiting access to urban amenities

45. **What is the potential benefit of implementing an IoT ecosystem in the industrial sector?**

    a. Increasing operational inefficiencies

    b. Reducing data collection and analysis

    c. Enabling predictive maintenance and real-time monitoring

    d. Eliminating the need for human workers

46. **How does the IoT ecosystem contribute to enhancing transportation systems?**

    a. By increasing traffic congestion

    b. By enabling real-time traffic monitoring and navigation

    c. By promoting higher fuel consumption

    d. By reducing the importance of public transportation

47. **How does the IoT ecosystem contribute to improving waste management?**

    a. By increasing littering and waste generation

    b. By enabling real-time monitoring of waste levels and collection

    c. By discouraging waste recycling efforts

    d. By promoting landfill usage

48. **How does the IoT ecosystem contribute to enhancing disaster management?**

    a. By increasing the impact of disasters

    b. By enabling real-time monitoring and early warnings

    c. By promoting unsafe practices during disasters

    d. By reducing the need for emergency response

49. **How does the IoT ecosystem contribute to enhancing public safety and security?**

    a. By promoting criminal activities

    b. By enabling real-time surveillance and emergency response

    c. By increasing privacy breaches

    d. By eliminating the need for security measures

50. **How does the IoT ecosystem contribute to enhancing retail operations?**

    a. By increasing stock shortages and customer dissatisfaction

    b. By enabling real-time inventory management and personalized shopping experiences

    c. By discouraging online shopping

    d. By reducing the need for customer data collection

51. **Which machine learning technique is particularly suited for classification tasks in IoT data analytics?**

    a. Linear regression

    b. K-means clustering

    c. Decision trees

    d. Principal component analysis (PCA)

52. **In the context of IoT system design, what does scalability refer to?**

    a. The ability of the system to handle increasing amounts of data or devices without performance degradation

    b. The ease of updating device firmware remotely

c. The capacity for real-time data processing

d. The level of data encryption supported

53. **Which of the following best describes the concept of data minimization in IoT privacy practices?**

a. Collecting only the data necessary for the intended purpose and discarding the rest

b. Encrypting all collected data

c. Reducing the frequency of data collection

d. Increasing data storage capacity

54. **Which approach is used to ensure high availability and reliability of IoT data storage systems?**

a. Data replication across multiple servers

b. Regular data backups

c. Cloud-based storage solutions

d. Local device storage

55. **In the context of IoT and AI, what does predictive analytics involve?**

a. Analyzing historical data to predict future events or trends

b. Monitoring real-time data for immediate responses

c. Classifying data into predefined categories

d. Performing sentiment analysis on user feedback

56. **What is a primary advantage of integrating IoT systems with cloud computing platforms?**

a. Increased local data storage capacity

b. Scalable data processing and storage resources

c. Enhanced device battery life

d. Improved physical device security

57. **Which cloud service model provides the most flexibility for deploying and managing IoT applications?**

a. Software as a service (SaaS)

b. Platform as a service (PaaS)

c. Infrastructure as a service (IaaS)

d. Function as a service (FaaS)

58. **Which technology is often used for urban traffic management in smart cities?**
    a. Li-Fi
    b. NFC
    c. Vehicle-to-everything (V2X)
    d. Zigbee

59. **What is a major challenge in deploying IoT solutions for smart city infrastructure?**
    a. Insufficient network bandwidth
    b. High device cost
    c. Integration of diverse data sources
    d. Lack of available IoT devices

60. **Which of the following is not typically a feature of IoT sensors?**
    a. Data collection
    b. Local data storage
    c. Data transmission
    d. Data processing

61. **What type of IoT device is designed to monitor environmental conditions such as temperature and humidity?**
    a. Actuator
    b. Gateway
    c. Sensor
    d. Controller

62. **Which network topology is characterized by devices connecting directly to each other without relying on a central hub?**
    a. Star topology
    b. Mesh topology
    c. Tree topology
    d. Bus topology

63. **What is the primary advantage of a star network topology in an IoT setup?**
    a. Increased fault tolerance
    b. Reduced network congestion
    c. Simplified network management
    d. Enhanced security features

64. **Which feature is commonly found in IoT-enabled wearable devices?**

    a. Heart rate monitoring

    b. High-resolution display screens

    c. Long-range communication

    d. Advanced data processing capabilities

65. **What is a primary challenge associated with the deployment of IoT wearable technology?**

    a. Limited network connectivity

    b. Battery life and power consumption

    c. Device size and weight

    d. High data processing requirements

66. **Which IoT application is commonly used to monitor soil moisture levels in precision agriculture?**

    a. Drone-based imaging

    b. Soil sensors

    c. Automated irrigation systems

    d. Weather forecasting tools

67. **What is the primary benefit of using IoT sensors for crop monitoring in agriculture?**

    a. Increased manual labor requirements

    b. Enhanced data accuracy for better crop management

    c. Reduced equipment costs

    d. Improved soil quality

Conclusion

This chapter is a comprehensive resource for individuals who are preparing for interviews in the swiftly evolving field of the IoT. The readers have encountered a diverse array of multiple-choice questions in this chapter, each of which is intended to assess their comprehension of both fundamental and advanced IoT concepts. These questions cover a broad range of topics, including architecture, communication protocols, security challenges, and real-world applications. The readers had the opportunity to enhance their understanding, identify areas that necessitate additional research, and acquire an understanding of the types of questions that are frequently posed by employers in this field by interacting with these enquiries. The chapter also underscores the significance of remaining informed about the latest technologies and trends in the IoT landscape, as the field is in a state of perpetual evolution. This chapter offers valuable preparation for readers, regardless of their level of experience or familiarity with IoT, to confidently respond to interview questions, showcase their expertise, and establish themselves as strong candidates in the competitive IoT job market. It will be essential for individuals who aspire to advance their professions and contribute to the ongoing development of this transformative industry to be well-prepared for interviews as the IoT continues to dictate the future of technology.

Join our Discord space

Join our Discord workspace for latest updates, offers, tech happenings around the world, new releases, and sessions with the authors:

https://discord.bpbonline.com

Answers

Q.No.	Answers
1	b
2	d
3	c
4	b
5	b
6	b
7	c
8	b
9	b
10	b
11	c
12	b
13	b
14	b
15	b
16	b
17	b
18	b
19	b
20	b
21	b
22	b
23	b
24	b
25	b
26	b
27	b
28	b
29	b
30	b

Q.No.	Answers
31	b
32	b
33	b
34	b
35	b
36	b
37	c
38	b
39	b
40	b
41	b
42	b
43	b
44	b
45	c
46	a
47	b
48	b
49	b
50	b
51	c
52	a
53	a
54	a
55	a
56	b
57	c
58	c
59	c
60	b

Q.No.	Answers
61	c
62	b
63	c
64	a
65	b
66	b
67	b

Join our Discord space

Join our Discord workspace for latest updates, offers, tech happenings around the world, new releases, and sessions with the authors:

https://discord.bpbonline.com